D1508045

THE **HUMAN AGENDA**

ALSO BY JOE WENKE

Looking for Potholes, Poems

The Talk Show, a Novel

Free Air, Poems

*Papal Bull: An Ex-Catholic Calls Out
the Catholic Church*

*You Got to Be Kidding! A Radical Satire
of The Bible*

Mailer's America

THE HUMAN AGENDA

Conversations
about
Sexual Orientation & Gender Identity

JOE WENKE

STAMFORD, CONNECTICUT   2015

Trans Über LLC
www.transuber.com

Copyright © 2015 by Joe Wenke

All rights reserved under International and Pan-American Copyright
Conventions. Published in the United States of America by Trans Über LLC,
Stamford, Connecticut.

No part of this book may be reproduced or transmitted in any form or by any
means, electronic or mechanical, including photocopy, recording, or any other
information storage and retrieval system, except for brief excerpts in a review
or essay referring to this book, without prior permission in writing from the
publisher.

To reach the author or Trans Über email: joewenke@joewenke.org

ISBN: 978-0-9863379-3-2

Digital editions available.

Manufactured in the United States of America
First Edition

DESIGN AND COMPOSITION: JOHN LOTTE / BLUE MOUNTAIN MARKETING
COVER ART DIRECTION AND HUMAN AGENDA LOGO DESIGN: MATT WOOD
COVER DESIGN: JOHN HAMILTON
FRONT COVER PHOTO: HANK SHIFFMAN

www.joewenke.org
Follow Joe Wenke on Twitter @joewenke.

For Mark, Ryan, Olivia and Gisele

@wenke

The homosexual agenda is the human agenda:
life, liberty and the pursuit of happiness. #LGBTQI

@wenke

The transgender agenda is the human agenda:
life, liberty and the pursuit of happiness. #LGBTQI

CONTENTS

PREFACE

This book has a really simple, innocent premise. I'm ready to debate anybody any time anywhere on the fact that it is just as natural and authentic to be LGBTQI as it is to be straight or cisgender. At the same time I recognize how difficult it is to change anybody's opinion on anything, let alone on issues of sexual orientation and gender identity. So I've decided with this book to take a different approach to advocacy. Specifically, I've put together a book that in its heart of hearts is really just a series of conversations in which people tell stories about themselves. In other words it's a book in which human beings share their life experiences. My hope is that by sharing stories about ourselves, we may create the possibility for understanding and empathy, where perhaps previously there was little or no understanding or empathy. My hope is that these stories may help to counteract the voices of ignorance and hate. Perhaps straight and cisgender readers with open minds and hearts who do not currently understand or embrace LGBTQI people will think to themselves, "You know, I've felt that way myself" or "Actually I see now that you have the same goals in life that I do." In fact, I'm hoping that all of my readers will experience similar epiphanies. Ultimately my hope is that my readers will find common ground with the amazing people who tell their stories in these pages and with me as well and that from the standpoint of that common ground, we will all recognize and celebrate our shared humanity.

AUTHOR'S NOTE

In THE HUMAN AGENDA various acronyms are used to refer to our community. The acronyms include respectively LGBTQI (i.e., lesbian, gay, bisexual, transgender, queer and intersex), LGBTQ, LGBTI and LGBT. These variations reflect the various ways that people in the community refer to the community.

I am hoping that we can move to a consensus on a non-acronym-based way to refer to the community, but we are clearly not there yet, and I do not personally have a solution. I would simply add that I am honored to have had the opportunity in working on this project to speak with such a diverse group of people and that the goal of these conversations is to be inclusive and to stand up for the values of freedom, justice and equality for all people.

KRISTIN RUSSO

"So many of these issues, as serious as they are, in so many cases really hinge on universal human needs."

Kristin Russo is co-founder along with Dannielle Owens-Reid of "Everyone Is Gay," which works to improve the lives of lesbian, gay, bisexual, transgender and questioning/queer youth. Together, they provide honest advice to kids while keeping them laughing; talk to students across the country in an effort to create caring, compassionate school environments and work with parents of LGBTQ kids to help foster an ongoing dialogue and a deeper understanding of life.

JOE: Kristin, what I find fascinating is that you're working in a communications medium that to me seems not just old school but positively moribund: it's the old advice column. As somebody from the baby boom generation, I know about it through Dear Abby and Ann Landers. And yet you and Dannielle have really transformed that genre. You've made it fresh and fun and real, so I'm wondering, did you have to evolve towards that goal? Obviously the style of "Everyone Is Gay" reflects your personalities, but was it like that day one? Was it like this Big Bang, and just like that you had completely re-invented the genre?

KRISTIN: Well when we started the site and began giving advice, our main objective was to be fun and funny. We really didn't have any concept of the fact that we would slowly begin to take on serious questions and address them in a way that incorporated lightheartedness in a style that hadn't been used before. Having said that, I don't know that we completely reinvented the wheel. When I first moved to New York City in 2000, I would pick up the *Village Voice* as often as I could so that I could read Dan Savage's column. His columns were hilarious and brutally honest. They had a very different tone. I really think they informed the way that I approached my writing. They helped me realize that I could say what I was feeling and also make people laugh about issues that might not always be hilarious to everyone.

JOE: It's so important to inject humor into your answers because you're dealing with really serious issues, life and death issues in some cases, and to have credibility and to be able to connect with people that you don't know otherwise, which raises another question: you seem to be so on point all the time, and yet practically speaking all you know about these people is what you have in their questions. How do you deal with that—the fact that you know so little and that you're dealing with such serious issues that touch the lives of young people who are trying to find themselves in terms of their sexual orientation and/or gender identity?

KRISTIN: I think that Dannielle and I have both approached this the same way since day one, which is that we've lived our lives and we have experience from having lived those lives that we draw upon. Also, I have a master's degree in gender studies, so that informs some of the way that I write and some of the way that I communicate too. But what we have found and what I think our entire movement is hinged on is that so many of these issues, as serious as they are, in so many cases really hinge on universal human needs. For example, that kid who is terrified to come out to his parents because he thinks he might get kicked out of his house. He isn't sure about XYZ. Yeah, there are specifics, and those specifics are rooted in sexuality, but at the end of the day most of us can understand what it is to have parents and what it is to be afraid of what your parents might think about a particular facet of your love life. So that's just really informed us, and it's really propelled us forward—just sort of accessing our own human experience and talking about it as clearly and concisely as we can.

JOE: Also, you call your project "Everyone is Gay," which is a self-evident truth. Everybody knows that's true, but I think it's cool that you came up with that. What exactly do you mean when you say, "Everyone is gay?"

KRISTIN: Well, complete transparency. When we named the website it was just a website, we didn't know it was going to turn into an organization.

JOE: It was just called "website" at first?

KRISTIN: Yeah, we started as a Tumblr, and Dannielle and I Gchatted one day and said to each other we should name it this funny thing or the other funny thing, and at the same moment she said, "No one is straight," and I said, "Everyone is gay," and then I got on the subway, and when I got above ground, she had texted me and said "It's up! I launched it. It's called 'Everyone is Gay.'" And so at first, it was just supposed to be funny, like tongue-in-cheek—"Everyone's gay." But now if somebody says I came out to my friends as trans, and they're being super supportive, but I don't know that they really understand it, and I feel misunderstood, it's like all right, so let's say, "Everyone is trans." On the other hand, let's say, "Everyone is gay" in the case of the kid who didn't want to come out to his parents as gay. What are you asking for in that case? You're really asking for the approval of your parents and for the acceptance and understanding of your friends. And so that's really what the name has come to mean to us now, but in its inception it was just for laughs.

JOE: What's interesting to me though is that you're really addressing the same kind of point that I'm trying to address in this project with the phrase, "The Human Agenda." The Human Agenda is actually an ironic commentary on the old hate speech phrase "the homosexual agenda." When I Tweet about that, I'll say, the homosexual agenda is the human agenda—it's life, liberty and the pursuit of happiness. In other words we're all people; we're all looking to achieve the same goals. And I say the same thing about the transgender agenda—that it's the human agenda. And so I think it's finding that common ground that provides an opportunity to communicate and to understand that is so important, particularly on issues of gender identity, which it disturbs me so deeply to say are still so little understood—I think even less understood than sexual orientation. Would you agree with that?

KRISTIN: Oh, absolutely, wholeheartedly. I think that trans people and trans issues are just now beginning to get the attention that they have deserved for a long time, and I think there's a really, really long road ahead for recognition and understanding of the trans experience.

JOE: Ian Harvie, who is a trans man stand-up comedian, is also participating in The Human Agenda project. He uses his experience as a trans man as a basis for much of his comedy just as you and Dannielle use your own life experiences as the basis for giving advice, and he has this bit in his act where he says you know I actually had to come out to my parents twice. First, as a girl, I told them one day, "you know, Mom and Dad, I like girls." And then the second time it was like, "well, Mom and Dad I still like girls, but guess what? I wanna be a dude." So it's true. Trans men and women often end up coming out twice to their parents, and, you know, you do have to think, what was that like for his parents just as much as what was that like for him.

KRISTIN: Mm-hmm.

JOE: So, it's an issue that I think is very difficult to address. What about, though, that whole issue of coming out and of families? You've started the Parents Project. I really would like to get an understanding from you about the extent to which you think families maybe are more supportive than they used to be when their kids come out, whether from a sexual orientation or gender identity standpoint. I mean you've spoken to tens of thousands of young people at this point and are in touch with parents and are traveling to schools around the country. If you were to take the pulse right now of what it is like in families and what it is like for kids to come out, what would you say?

KRISTIN: You know, I think that there's definitely a difference mostly in the knowledge category when it comes to parents. I think since I came out to my parents, I don't know, God, fifteen years ago or something like that, I think there are more parents who are a bit more educated on what life might look like for their LGBTQ kid in the future, so I think that helps. But in terms of taking the pulse of the young people who have to do the coming out, it doesn't seem different at all. The fear and the uncertainty and the confusion about how to talk about this with parents are just as present. It's identical to how it was, you know, fifteen years ago. We have so many young people who, when they talk about their parents, it's very plain that their parents are very accepting, very open-minded, but still they're just terrified. So many kids think that even though their parents are open-minded and understand issues, it will be different when it's their kid and so that fear is still really, really alive in the lives of many young people.

JOE: Well, I would think that it's a fundamental issue for caring, loving parents. If you know your child is gay or lesbian or transgender, you're going to worry about them being persecuted for that. You're going to worry about them being bullied at school. How do you deal with that issue, both from a kid perspective and a parent perspective, the whole issue of bullying?

KRISTIN: Well, you know, that's a really tricky question to unpack. Dannielle and I have a new book called *This is a Book for Parents of Gay Kids* that goes hand in hand with the Parents Project. It's our first foray into really talking about bullying and trying to talk about bullying from the parents' perspective. So many of the things that I had read online were logical on paper. They seemed to make sense like—these are the steps that you take, and you should make sure that XYZ knows, and in some cases maybe you have a great school administration, and maybe they know exactly how to handle the situation, and maybe those steps will work, but it seemed like there was a lot of the reality missing—for example, the fact that you're going to have some serious fears and feelings about this, the fact that your kid might not want you to approach the school administration, and so I would say to a parent who's dealing with that, the first step is always to talk to your kid, because your kid is on the front lines. Your kid is the one that's in that school, and they know. They know the teachers who are going to be their allies. They know the teachers who are not, and I think being able to have an open dialogue, as open as possible with your kid, is always the first step. If you're afraid that your kid is in danger and your kid won't talk to you, then obviously you have to take action on your own, but I think a lot of parents kind of discredit the knowledge that their kids have about what's going on in that situation and go right to the administration or teachers. I think it's important to start with the young person first.

JOE: I think what's disturbing too is that bullying goes on throughout life for people in the LGBTQ community. I did a piece for the *Huffington Post* focused on transgender women called "That's a Man!" And it had to do with the fact that it's really literally still dangerous to walk down the street if you are an LGBTQ person, even in a progressive city like New York. For example, there was a transgender woman, Islan Nettles, who was killed when she was walking down the street with some friends in Harlem in the summer of 2013. The killing actually occurred in front of a police precinct. Her attacker still has not been brought to justice. Also, Mayor Bloomberg came out and said that although hate crimes were significantly reduced in New York City, they had more than doubled with respect to the LGBTQ community. And so you have these issues continuing throughout life and for that reason they're just so difficult to deal with. Do you find apart from family, that a lot of the kids you're dealing with do have peers at least that they can talk to? Do they have outlets to confide their feelings about themselves and their hopes and their fears?

KRISTIN: A lot of them do. I think that the presence of gay-straight alliances in middle schools and high schools is much greater than it was years ago. Also, we're seeing more of a presence of queer characters in television and in movies. So there's more ability for young people to dialogue with their peers about some of these issues. But I think that the presence of the Internet is really one of the biggest steps in allowing young people to talk about their questions and their fears because even knowing that your friends maybe accept you and you've come out as bisexual and everything's cool, it doesn't really give you a complete outlet to ask the questions you really have, because you feel silly or you feel like maybe you're supposed to know already. And so I think that the space of the Internet, being able to Google things, is really important, and, you know, Tumblr is a huge community. We have people answering questions for each other, and you can ask things anonymously, and there is such a community there that I think it bridges what is lacking in peer-to-peer conversations.

JOE: Can you talk a little bit more about your book for parents?

KRISTIN: Sure, absolutely. It was sort of a no brainer for us to make the next step of "Everyone Is Gay" be dialogue with parents whose kids had just come out to them. So many of the questions that we get both through our site and when we tour schools are about either heart break and relationships or coming out to parents or explaining terminology to parents. For example, a parent might understand what "gay" means, but they might have no idea what the terms "queer" or "gender queer" mean. There are a lot of terms, and parents are trying to keep up. Also, we're struggling to keep up with some of the age-old questions, like is this my fault? Did I do something wrong to cause my child to be gay? After Dannielle and I talked about it a bit, we decided we would put our resources together and our own experience with our families together and write a book. When we looked online for resources for parents, we didn't find much. PFLAG (http://community. pflag.org/) has a great presence within communities, but other than that, there wasn't a strong presence of videos and collected advice for parents who have these pretty common questions. So we decided we would create it because we wanted to put something in the back of the book for parents to find online, and that's where the Parents Project was born. So it will include articles from experts, advice from Dannielle and me, advice from other parents, conversations with youth and coming out stories. It will include a large video library that we'll be building as well for parents that will help them find resources in their communities.

JOE: And you're also on YouTube.

KRISTIN: Yeah, we're on YouTube, and we're also working with some other people in the community. For example, a friend of ours, Lauren, identifies as trans, and she's doing a bunch of advice questions in video format that are more related to trans issues.

JOE: You mentioned the word "queer" a moment ago. I'd like to talk a little bit about the language of self-identification. The language is, of course, self-validating. I wonder what your point of view is though on the use of the word "queer," which seems not only to refer to sexual orientation but to gender identity. Do you think that word is being success- fully reinvented, and do you think that it's being used clearly? I have a Ph.D. in English, and I have to be honest. I find that it's used by different people in different ways all the time, and I find myself being a little bit confused by it—that is to say, people who are trans using that term or people who are gen- der fluid in addition to people who are lesbian or gay. What's your take on the use of that word?

KRISTIN: Well, you're just full of the hard questions. I come from an academic background where I took courses on Queer Theory, so I've been around the use of that word in so many different contexts, and I do find it to be really powerful be- cause so many of the other words that we use are a little bit more limited in what they define, although again that's changing every day. But for me personally I identify as a fe- male, and I am married to a woman who identifies as a fe- male. And so the word "lesbian" you'd think would fit for me.

I don't know why, but the word "lesbian" doesn't ever make me feel exactly right. It doesn't seem to fit who I am, and that's because of my own experience with that word. But the word "queer" to me means a lot more than that. It speaks to me more—more than just to my sexuality, but also to the general way that I operate in my day-to-day life. When I think of the word "queer" and how expansive it can be, I think, for example, of a friend of mine who lives in Virginia and rides freight trains as a mode of transportation and also as a way of having fun. It's this totally underground society where they have timetables, and they can find the trains and ride on those trains, and there's something to me that's inherently queer about the way my friend lives his life. He identifies as a man, and he's married to a woman, but he lives really outside of the grid that I think a lot of us are expected to live within. And so to me that's my understanding of the word "queer," and I think that it's really great for people to be able to access a word that doesn't have very stringent demarcations.

JOE: Right.

KRISTIN: It can be a little confusing, but I kind of think that's the fun of it, and that's an example of the positive things that are happening with the reclaiming of that word. But it's so personal, you know. It's all so personal.

JOE: It is personal, but you just brought out I think a really interesting connotation of the word—that it means being subversive.

KRISTIN: Exactly.

JOE: Undermining stereotypes or conventions. I think that is very powerful. But I think it's a very mixed bag when you try to reclaim words, like the use of the word "nigger." You know some people think if you're white, you don't even have the right to comment on that. But I'm not sure that using "n-i-g-g" with the "a" on the end is really the most positive way for people to refer to themselves. There are other words too, you know, like how "queen" is used. And so it's a very complicated topic. For example, wondering about what your audience is interpreting when you use those words. Also, the religious right haters of the LGBTQ community will latch on to absolutely anything. I mean there's just a constant echo chamber of hate from that group. If you go on Right Wing Watch, for example, every single day you'll find some sort of atrocity. And so I do think we have to be mindful of audience when we use these words, but you make a very strong case for the use of the word "queer" as a powerful term. How about when it's applied to gender as in "gender queer," what is your feeling about that?

KRISTIN: Just a comment on what you were saying a moment ago. I do think that it's really important when we use the words to be respectful of the people around us because if I were in a room and I used the word "queer" and somebody in that room came up to me and said, "You know that word really makes me very uncomfortable. Thirty years ago that word was used to hurt me badly, and there's no way for me to detach those feelings from that word," I would respect that person and their experience, and I would not use that word around them because I think that it is really personal. But in terms of using "queer" to attach it to gender, I mean I think "gender queer" to me makes a ton of sense. I know that if you're not familiar with the term, of course, it might not make any sense, but gender queer means that you're not necessarily identifying within the gender binary. Again you're talking about being subversive and breaking outside of a mold that is pre-existing. And I think that for that idea it's really powerful. And you know "gender queer" is a phrase again that can be confusing because if I say I'm gender queer and the person sitting next to me says they're gender queer, we may mean two completely different things, but you know it's probably better if you to have to have a conversation about what your identity means than if there's one term that you think answers all the questions for you.

JOE: Maybe the confusion is a good thing because I think part of the message is that the bifurcated view, that simplistic view of sexual orientation or gender identity, just isn't true. It's not true to people's experiences, and our experiences of ourselves are self-validating, and how we describe ourselves is entirely up to us. But your point, I think, is that we do have to be sensitive about audience and so people who are a little bit older may well have been hurt by the use of the word "queer." The whole purpose is communication to begin with, and I think we just need to be sensitive to that, and you and Dannielle certainly are. I'm just amazed at how on point you are with the advice that you give almost every single time. Have you ever felt after giving advice that you said something that you wish you hadn't said, and then you had to go back and change it? Have you ever followed up in your communication with somebody who asked you a question?

KRISTIN: Yeah, we have. It's hard for me to remember the specific incidences, but I'm almost certain that the majority of the times—there haven't been a ton—but the majority of times that we've posted something and then followed up the next day or later that day with some clarification or more of our thoughts has been directly related to gender. Talking about gender is really, really tricky. Neither Dannielle nor I identify as trans. Obviously we both have experiences with gender. You know, anyone on the planet does, but because of the fact that we don't identify as trans, it can be limiting to how much we can speak on that, and we've had a couple of occasions where we've said something that we didn't realize was possibly offensive to certain people. And Tumblr is a very vocal community. They let you know right away if you've said something that's upsetting, and in the majority of those cases when we looked at what they were saying, we were like, well damn, they're absolutely correct, and so we used it as a tool to sort of expand the conversation, and since all these incidences happened, Dannielle and I have grown a lot as people. We've also expanded our "panelists." For example, we have three different trans writers who address issues that we feel will be better addressed by somebody who is within the trans community.

JOE: Yes, so you have expanded your resources to include quite a few other people. Do you edit what they have to say, or do you just let them give advice?

KRISTIN: No, we very rarely edit, although it does happen. Recently one of our panelists answered a question that was very complex, and so she had to write a pretty long answer. And so we looked at it, and we just sent it back to her with a couple of additional sentences. They didn't necessarily need to be there, and then she sent it back and said this is totally fine. I approve. So we hardly ever edit anything, and if we do, it's always sent to the writer for their approval before it posts on the site. I mean that's the whole point of the project. It's that we're giving a voice to these other experiences, not to alter them in any way.

JOE: Right, not to control the response, but to allow these points of view to live and to be communicated.

KRISTIN: Exactly.

JOE: Well, that's really to me the whole spirit of what you're doing, and one of the reasons why you're so successful. You have such credibility. You base your advice on the truths that you've learned in your own lives and the authenticity that you have, and you're just making a tremendous contribution. So thanks so much for spending a little bit of time with me today and sharing.

KRISTIN: Thank you. You too! And thank you for all of the work that you are doing and continue to do. It's been a real pleasure.

JOE: My pleasure.

ANDREW **SOLOMON**

"I think there is a tyranny of the norm. . . . But actually what science indicates is that diversity is what strengthens a society or a culture or a species."

Andrew Solomon is a writer and lecturer on politics, culture and psychology as well as an activist in LGBTQ rights, mental health, education and the arts. His latest book, *Far From the Tree: Parents, Children and the Search for Identity,* has won many awards, including the National Book Critics Circle Award for Nonfiction. His previous book, *The Noonday Demon: An Atlas of Depression,* won the 2001 National Book Award for Nonfiction.

———————

JOE: Andrew, it's an honor to chat with you today.

ANDREW: It's a pleasure. Thank you.

JOE: *Far From the Tree* addresses a profound question: Is difference the foundation of human identity even if the difference-making element is a disability or is widely denigrated or pathologized? In your opening chapter entitled, "Son," you make an extraordinary connection between your experience growing up gay and people who are Deaf, which establishes the thesis of the book. I was wondering if you would talk a little bit about how you made that connection.

ANDREW: In about 1994, my editors at *the New York Times Magazine* asked me to write a piece about Deaf culture, and I was very taken aback. I had thought of deafness as a disability and had no sense of it as a culture. Then I went into the Deaf world—to Deaf theatre, Deaf clubs, the National Association of the Deaf meeting, the Miss Deaf America contest—and I came away thinking this is a culture, and while it's not my culture, it's a very beautiful culture. There were moments when I thought, "Gee, it would be fun to be one of these Deaf people and part of this world of people united by the shared use of sign language." Then I discovered that most deaf children are born to hearing parents and that those parents have tended historically to emphasize oral skills—the ability to lip-read and to use oral speech. As a result, many of those children don't discover Deaf culture until their adolescence, when it comes as a great revelation to them and gives them, finally, a sense of identity. And it just struck me that that trajectory so paralleled the experience of gay children who are mostly born to straight parents who mostly think that straight lives are in general happier than gay ones and who often pressure their children to conform to the straight world—with the result that the children discover gay culture only in adolescence or thereafter when they are very much liberated by it. So I saw real parallels between those two experiences.

JOE: What's striking to me is that relatively few people with the ability to hear would say that hearing is essential to their human identity, although hearing is certainly part of what makes us human. But as you point out, a Deaf person may well view their deafness as essential to their identity and as the identifying element of their participation in a culture. What is it about difference that makes it so definitive of our core beings, of our human identity?

ANDREW: Well, I think the ways in which we correspond to the mainstream, to the dominant part of society, are less noticeable. They don't define our identity, because identity derives from the ways in which you are specific and particular and different from other people. So anything exceptional, either positive or negative, will become your identity.

JOE: Difference is clearly the foundation of identity, but at the same time, differences can form the basis for bigotry and discrimination.

ANDREW: People are frightened of difference, and therefore it often does form the basis for exactly that—bigotry and discrimination.

JOE: In the book you share so many stories of how families respond when they have children who are different. Many of the stories are both inspiring and heartbreaking. What would you say you learned about family in relation to your own experience as a husband and a father?

ANDREW: I formulated the idea that there are different kinds of identity: vertical identities that get passed down generationally from parent to child, such as ethnicity and nationality, and horizontal identities that occur when people are different from their parents. I think the experience of looking at different kinds of horizontal identities has informed my fatherhood, giving me the sense that my children are not going to be a replication of me. They're going to be their own people. They're going to be separate and distinct. Part of the process of fatherhood has to be to change your children. You have to educate them. You have to teach them manners. You have to instill moral values. But part of the process of parenting is also to celebrate your children for who they are. I'm awake to the need to identify who they are and to help them feel good about it, more awake because of my encounters with so many parents who were faced with children whom in the abstract they would have thought they couldn't love but who then rose to the occasion of loving them.

JOE: One of your chapters focuses on transgender people, and of course being transgendered is not a disease or a disorder, despite being pathologized by the medical community, as homosexuality once was. As you make clear in the book, identity is self-validating. We're all entitled to the tautology of identity. And yet transgender people are among the most denigrated and marginalized people on the planet. Why do you think that being transgendered creates such a deep, visceral, negative reaction in so many people and as in fact homosexuality still does as well?

ANDREW: I tried to investigate that as I wrote the book, and I was astonished by the level of hatred that the trans people I interviewed had been subjected to. It was truly appalling, and some of the stories in the book are devastating. I think that people are most comfortable when the world is orderly. I think there's the sense that when you begin questioning basic distinctions, such as the distinction between being male and being female, it represents a threat to the social order. And I think most people are at some level insecure in their own gender identity or in their own sexuality and that they therefore find it very difficult to deal with people who are different. I also think that people target those whom they perceive to be different and weak. Historically people who are trans have not had enormous power. People who are gay have not had enormous power.

JOE: To some extent it's an opportunistic attack on the vulnerable, the weak, the disenfranchised, the marginalized.

ANDREW: Exactly.

JOE: But do you also think that moral judgments about homosexuality, or for that matter being transgendered, though they're often justified by religion, might actually be motivated by a desire to eradicate difference, while championing a kind of tyranny of the norm?

ANDREW: I think there is a tyranny of the norm. It's no coincidence that the most effective attack on gay people was when they were targeted during the Third Reich. Hitler went after gay people as much as he did after the Jews. Some people think that you can purify a society and that it will be stronger. But actually what science indicates is that diversity is what strengthens a society or a culture or a species. Diversity is what actually leaves people best adapted to pursue the things they need to pursue in life.

JOE: Well, you've written a profound book. I think in telling the incredibly moving stories of people who are different and the families who love and care for them, you've succeeded in telling the story of life itself. That is an amazing achievement. So I thank you, Andrew, for spending a few minutes with me today.

ANDREW: It's been a real pleasure. Thank you so much.

AIDAN KEY

"This concept of gender identity is the real paradigm-shifting piece. Can you accept that gender identity exists and that for most people gender identity will align with their anatomical sex, but for some it doesn't? That's the question to walk out the door and consider, because if you can accept that, then we have a whole new way of considering things."

Aiden Key is the founder and director of Gender Diversity Education and Support Services, which is based in Seattle. The mission of Gender Diversity is to increase awareness and understanding of the wide range of gender variations in children, adolescents and adults by providing family support, building a community of awareness, increasing awareness within society and improving the lives of people of all gender identities and expressions. In addition to working with transgender and gender variant children, adolescents and their families, Aidan is also very active in creating awareness and understanding of gender identity issues in schools, in the workplace and among healthcare professionals.

———————

JOE: Aidan, it's great to speak with you today.

AIDAN: Thank you so much.

JOE: I was wondering if we could begin by your sharing with me how you first became involved in working with transgender children and their families. What led you to that vocation and that mission?

AIDAN: Nothing led me to it. They came to me. I was busy navi-
gating my personal journey, my own gender exploration and
how to find my way when there was no path. Much of that
exploration resulted in my early organizing work, which included the Gender Odyssey Conference, where I first met
parents of transgendered children. At the time I did not have
programming for them. Frankly, I just did not believe that
kind of support was possible. My belief was that everyone
needed to somehow make it to adulthood, where they could
then embark on their own journey. So I was delighted and
surprised and at a loss as to how to help these families who
wanted support for their children.

JOE: So would you say that your own experiences discovering
your own gender identity led you naturally into this work
now?

AIDAN: Oh, absolutely and not so much as a conscious choice
to do work and engage in activism but to maintain connections. The little bit that I knew of a transgendered person's
life was that it involved an incredible amount of loss. Loss
of family, friends, children, jobs, sometimes housing—so
much loss. I was really aware of this as I was embarking on
my own journey and desperate to keep as many people in
my life as I could. So my first organizing was just pulling together folks within friendships and families and sharing my
experience, my confusion, my hopes, my fears, all of that.
And I found that there was some great success with that approach. Then I began to transform that effort into a small
community event here and there, growing into multiple community events and then ultimately a conference and onward
from there.

JOE: Well, there are undoubtedly a wide range of emotions that
families experience—mothers, fathers, siblings—when a

child begins to self-identify as transgender. It's obviously a great challenge. Could you just give a little bit of the sense of the range of emotions that families go through and what their responses are to having a child who self-identifies as transgender?

AIDAN: Yes. I've yet to meet a parent who was delighted to discover that they have a transgender or gender-nonconforming child. Without exception, I would say that they are confused. Many of them are unfamiliar with what being transgender means, having been provided with only negative images in society and the media. It's a challenge for them to connect the little they do know with their child whom they love and know very well. So it's quite a significant barrier for them. By the time I meet them, they've at least articulated this either to themselves, to a spouse or partner or to a provider out there in the world, trying to find some type of resource that could shed some light on this for them. That's about when they arrive in my world.

JOE: It's positive, of course, that they're reaching out for that knowledge, that education, that support from you.

AIDAN: Right. I think that's an incredible amount to work with, and I know that that moment they pick up the phone or send that email or walk through the door for a support group is a pretty critical moment. The environment that's created, how the other families receive them, how I engage with them in those first few moments can mean the difference between them continuing to engage or perhaps never coming back. And so that's the foundation that I base my groups on and the foundation that I offer up to facilitators I'm training for my other groups, that initial contact is such a critical place— for example, if a parent is angry that their teen is saying, "I'm gender queer" and using language that's really unfamiliar to them. A parent may view that as a child attempting to get attention or to get a rise out of them or do something that would just get their goat, so to speak. There can be a lot of denial from parents about what is indeed reality for their child. A number of them say things like, "Well, it started when my kid went to this camp with other kids and started hanging out with these other kids who are like this. They wouldn't have done that otherwise," as if it's contagious in some way. But regardless of the reasons that they come up with, every last one of them is afraid. They're afraid for their child. They care about and love their child. They want their child to have a good life. They want their child to have a safe life. They want their child to be loved and accepted and to do well in society. And everything in their fiber says that this will prevent them from having any of those things, including even their own lives.

JOE: Well, I know too that some parents actually experience a sense of loss when their child begins identifying as transgender. I mean, for example, if their child was born male, they may feel that they're losing a son or if the child is born female, they may feel that they're losing a daughter. How do you deal with that kind of an emotion when, of course, in fact the child is still there, but there is this sense of grief or loss in addition to the other fears that they rightly have about their child's safety?

AIDAN: Occasionally there's a family that doesn't, but most of them will experience grief. That's actually a second stage when they're at a place of acceptance. Once acceptance comes, immediately the grief comes too. And it absolutely can feel like the death of their child. When parents have any of these emotions, whether it's anger, fear or grief, it's so important to create that space for them to feel absolutely that way and validate those emotions, that feeling of loss. There is loss. There is loss for any adult person doing a gender transition, and many of us can articulate those losses. We also have gains, and we do our best to focus on the positive things that it brings into our lives and to empower ourselves that way. But I believe quite strongly that the best way to help these parents help their children is to create that space for that loss, for that fear, for that anger and not try to move them through it or excuse it away or challenge them.

JOE: Yes. It's legitimate and it's real and it's not to be denied or rationalized in any way, so you need to give it space.

AIDAN: But you would be surprised how even other parents who were in the same place the year before will out of their own discomfort or even in an effort to help just excuse it away rather than make space for it. Simply because they want to offer that hope, which is great, but there's no way out but through, as they say.

JOE: Absolutely. Turning to another issue, Aiden, another reason that the work you're doing is so important is that it demonstrates that children self-identify at a very young age as transgender. And I'm wondering in those very young children how often you observe what psychologists call "dysphoria," that is, a discomfort with the bodies they were born in as opposed to the child simply identifying as transgender in a kind of natural way. Do you really see dysphoria in very young children, or are they simply being themselves and then perhaps feel anxiety or discomfort when they're not supported?

AIDAN: It's been an incredible learning experience to work with these families and to see some recurring themes coming out. Parents have told me, "As soon as my child was able to talk, they were correcting me on how I referred to their gender." So their son is saying, "I am not a boy. I am a girl." This is not every child, but it is some children. So some children from a very early age with their brilliant learning capacity and the sponges that they are—they're taking in what they know and have already experienced about gender, and when they're able to form words, they're articulating who they are. What happens pretty immediately is that they are told they're incorrect. And it can be by the most loving parents, by babysitters, by siblings, by extended family, by neighbors, you name it. There's a mountain of pushback against this small child.

JOE: Instantaneous pushback, like, "Oh, you're making a mistake. You're obviously a little boy. You're not a girl."

AIDAN: Yes, you're confused. What I hear from the majority of these parents is that the most common age of early identification is between six and seven. What I've also learned is that there's oftentimes a lot more fluidity provided up through kindergarten. But by the time first or second grade comes around, there's definitely a delineation that is supported by the peers and supported by the teachers. In neighborhoods, playgrounds, families, and so on. The really cute, isn't that adorable cross gender exploration is now not acceptable. And that's when a child starts experiencing distress. And that's what society will look at and say, "Oh, that child is gender dysphoric." So is there a problem with the child or a problem with the fact that the child can't find a place to fit into society as who they are? I believe that's more the crux of it than anything else. There's also a lack of language to describe who they are. Those children who can articulate their gender identity to others at a very young age are a percentage of the kids. The children who don't have that language can't even remember how young they were when they first realized that who they are does not fit with how others perceive them.

JOE: But, as you've said, in some children it goes back almost to the beginning of when they can communicate that they express a self-identification with being transgendered. And so to me it's evident that being transgendered is natural, in the same sense that being cisgender is. And whether one wants to look to nature or nurture, it's simply part of what I would call a normal, natural development for some children. And yet it's true that mental health professionals continue to pathologize being transgendered—formerly, categorizing transgender people as having a gender identity disorder and now using this so-called kinder, gentler term "dysphoria," but still acting as if there's something wrong with you if you're transgendered. And of course back in the day, the same kind of labeling was applied to people who are gay. In your work with mental health professionals, how do you address this view? I see videos on the Internet with very well intended health care professionals still using this term "dysphoria" to diagnose transgender children. Of course, health professionals also argue that transgender people need treatment and that unless there's a diagnosis, they're not going to get the proper treatment. But there doesn't seem to be any reason to pathologize people for being who they are. So how do you deal with that in the mental health community?

AIDAN: You just don't ask the simple questions, do you?

JOE: Well, it's very troubling to me because I think that transgender people carry this stigma inside themselves that even professionals, therapists, for example, think that you have something wrong with you, and so they treat you rather than acknowledging you as having discovered your identity. Rather than saying the way you feel is authentic, they view being transgendered as a problem that needs to be treated. Clearly when there is so little understanding and support, transgendered people are going to feel uncomfortable. Anyone feels uncomfortable when they're not supported and when they're not understood. But, as you're implying, that's because of the lack of understanding, the ignorance within society, not because if you are transgendered, there is necessarily a problem that you need therapy for.

AIDAN: Right. Imagine if you could place yourself in a transgendered person's body and experience from day one everything they ever encountered that told them that who they innately are and who they feel themselves to be in the world is absolutely wrong. They are told they are confused at best, perverted and sick at worst. And yet you find those people as adults who have survived that journey to adulthood, and have then said "You know what? Come hell or high water, I need to be authentic. I need to be myself. I need to address this issue. I will get there in whatever way I can and explore every path that I can or carve the path if there is none." What those adults have done for quite a number of years is encounter those providers who don't have the capacity to understand that experience, who may want to help but really have no idea how, but who provide them with authorization, perhaps to open the door to hormone care, surgical intervention, document changes, whatever it might be. And what transgendered people have done is to share that information. Hey, I found one person in the United States who we can go to, to help us. And here are the limitations this person has. So I was successful when I went in and told them a, b, and c. So I suggest that you go in and say a, b, and c. So we continue to do that. We are definitely expanding and moving into d, e, and f and continuing down the line to provide the providers with the understanding they need of the complexity of our experiences. But the foundation has been established on some very rudimentary elements. That's the foundation for our medical and our mental health viewpoints. Now you add children into the mix. This is definitely changing, but we know the narrative. I am a man trapped in a woman's body. I wish to change my body. I have this type of distress. At one point, our gender transitions even needed to result in a heterosexual orientation, or we were not identified as true transsexuals.

JOE: Really.

AIDAN: That's still going on. In other countries especially. Absolutely. So that's the foundation, and it's not a long history. We're talking what, '40s, '50s, '60s, '70s. There are providers who have informed the field of knowledge who are still engaged in the field and are the leaders. So they have their truths and have established a body of knowledge based on their truths. But we're watching a lot of people become empowered and actually say, "Huh, that's not quite right for me. My journey is unique. My economic background influenced my life in this way. My racial identity influenced my life in another way." Family support or no family support. Career choices. Everything informs how a person's going to move through. And there are many factors that can put us on the fringe and marginalize us—housing or jobs and so on. But there is more of a re-examination now. No matter where I go, if it's doctors, psychiatrists, parents, teachers, social workers—they're all in the same place. So oftentimes I will start by saying, this is how we've approached this in the past, and we have approached it this way out of a place of love and support. But when we're looking at an adult population that has a 41% attempted suicide rate, it's not working. So now what we're saying is OK, we tried to get people to conform to societal expectation. With respect to children it might be taking the dolls and the dresses and so forth away from the boy. Encouraging the girl to be more feminine, engage in more feminine activities and so forth. Now we say, "Let's support these children," and it's almost like a question. Everybody's looking at each other and saying, "Should we support these children in who they are, in who they say they are?" And everybody's looking at each other and kind of saying, "Well, I don't know. I mean it seems like that could be a good thing to do." But none of us knows how to do it. What does a world look like that allows some fluidity, trying this on or that on, allowing that one day you might feel more female and another day you might feel more male. Is that OK? Is that dangerous? Is that harmful? Ultimately, it's harmful when this society does not make room for that.

JOE: Exactly.

AIDAN: When we change the systems—whether that's the family system or the school system, the neighborhood and so on—when we change the environments around the child to allow for that, these kids thrive. And they grow and they navigate their gender. Now definitely there are a number of people who have a disconnect with their physical bodies. But the beauty about supporting a child early is that by the time those physical decisions come into place, that child has had the opportunity to explore and find their best fit. We could surely benefit from studies of children who are supported in their gender exploration. And based on what I've seen with now several hundred families, it appears that a high percentage of these kids continue to grow and thrive in their innate gender identity that does not align with their anatomical sex. That's with support systems in place. The other thing to consider when educating those who are not transgender and those who are unfamiliar with this issue but want to learn more is to encourage them to stretch their brains, to consider the concept of gender fluidity. That it's not only male and female.

JOE: Yes, that gender identity exists along a spectrum. It's not a binary issue.

AIDAN: When I'm leading a presentation, I say that this concept of gender identity is the real paradigm-shifting piece.

Can you accept that gender identity exists and that for most people gender identity will align with their anatomical sex, but for some it doesn't. That's the question to walk out the door and consider, because if you can accept that, then we have a whole new way of considering things. Also to consider whether gender identity could have a fluid development over time? Or what informs that gender identity? Of course, in every presentation, I have to differentiate gender identity from sexual orientation. And that can take a bit of work, because again I think people can understand that on an intellectual level but not on a gut level.

JOE: I'm glad that you brought that up, Aidan. You're quoted by Andrew Solomon in his very important book, *Far from the Tree: Parents, Children and the Search for Identity*, on that precise topic. And you make the distinction between gender identity and sexual orientation by saying, "My gender is who I am. My sexuality is who I bounce it off of." And, as you say in the book, this confusion between gender identity and sexual orientation may provide a glimpse into why people are threatened by gender identity insofar as they seem to relate it to sexuality that they don't accept as well. And so the two issues are kind of mixed up together.

AIDAN: Absolutely. This is a topic of conversation that is much discussed within the trans community. That gender identity and sexual orientation are two very distinct components of who we are. So we can pull them apart intellectually. But as adults we realize they are inextricable in how we move forward in life, in how we engage with people. If I meet someone who I perceive to be female and heterosexual and she perceives me to be male and heterosexual, she's going to engage with me in a certain way. She's going to keep a certain distance depending on a number of factors. Because she knows that however she engages with me sends me messages as to whether I should come closer or whether I should keep a distance. And we are doing that kind of dance with everyone. If I'm interacting with a man, does he perceive me to be homosexual? And what does that mean to him and his identity?

JOE: Sexual orientation and gender identity are distinct but also very closely bound together, and what's interesting is that both of these issues seem to be threatening to people, what one's gender identity is, particularly if it's nonconforming, or what one's sexual orientation is if one is not heterosexual, if one is gay or lesbian or queer or bisexual, even in my own case. I'm very attracted to transgender women. There isn't even a word to describe that sexual orientation as if transgender women don't exist.

AIDAN: Well, it already got used. The logical word would be "transsexual."

JOE: Right.

AIDAN: If you think of the words, "heterosexual," "homosexual" and "bisexual," an attraction to trans people would be "transsexual," right? But it's already been used, inappropriately in my opinion. But anyway, yes, definitely the threatening component is there. We do bring that component of sexual orientation to our engagements, but with children, it's different, because they're not at that place in life. They may have an awareness of their attractions. I believe that young children can have a sense of their attractions to other people and their sexual orientation, but they're not doing anything about it until they're adolescents in most circumstances. So if I can make that distinction in my training with providers, with teachers, then I've helped them remember what gender meant when they were children. And what gender means when we are children is what type of tennis shoes or jeans or backpacks do we select? What activities do we engage in and who are our friends? When adults remember that, clarity is significantly improved, and their ability to then move forward is significantly improved. When I speak to professionals, I don't provide them with medical expertise. I'm not a trained teacher. I'm not a social worker. I'm not any of these things. They have those tools. If I can move them to this place of remembrance, then they know how to grab their tools and apply them in a new way and begin to create that gender expansive environment. And transgender children just naturally benefit from that.

JOE: In his book, Andrew Solomon examines people who are different from the general population for very different reasons. For example, he focuses on deaf people, dwarves, schizophrenic people, people on the autism spectrum, people with Down syndrome and transgender people, and he examines how families deal with those differences. In doing this, he poses a critical question: to what extent are those differences viewed as an identity or as a disorder? And I think the profound point that he makes is that we all have a right to what he suggests is the tautology of self-identification. If I say I am transgender or if I say I am gay, my declaration demands respect. It has integrity. It has authenticity. It should not be viewed as a pathology or a problem. And maybe that's the breakthrough insight that people need to come to. You take people at their word when they say who they are.

AIDAN: Right. And that's what we're bumping up against. Do we have the right to say, "I am." I believe we do. Does society have a place for us? Well, not necessarily. With the people that he writes about, that's the common thread. Also, there is the issue of privilege. I find that if I can articulate gender privilege for the majority of the population who've never thought of that as even existing, then they have a framework to relate it to. It's no mystery to me that oftentimes in classroom discussions people of color click with these concepts more quickly. They have a parallel example in their own lives to relate it to. Like, "Oh that sounds a lot like what I experience," including what it's like day in day out, the daily microaggressions that can happen, that those who are in the area of privilege will invalidate, and say "Oh, no, I didn't mean anything bad by that. Of course, I don't see skin color. Skin color doesn't matter." Well skin color matters for the person of color who experiences hardships on a daily basis. So some people will say that about gender, "Oh, I don't see gender. I just see the person." I don't know. That sounds like a place of privilege. Maybe you should take a little closer look.

JOE: Well, you're really speaking to the point of this whole project that I'm doing. The reason I call it The Human Agenda is captured in a statement that I Tweet from time to time. I make the statement: The homosexual agenda—that horrible hate phrase—is really the human agenda: Life, liberty and the pursuit of happiness. And the transgender agenda is the same. Life, liberty and the pursuit of happiness. In other words, we all want the same things, and we all want respect. We all want to be embraced and maybe even be celebrated for who we are. And I think in your work, you are moving so many people to that realization and that awareness. It's such important work, and I really thank you for spending this time with me today. It's been very enlightening and inspiring. So thank you so much, Aidan and thank you for the work that you do.

AIDAN: Absolutely, absolutely, it's my pleasure.

GISELE ALICEA
(AKA GISELE XTRAVAGANZA)

"Transgender people are real people. We have mothers. We have fathers. We have sisters. We have brothers. We have families. We have somewhere that we came from."

Gisele Alicea, aka Gisele Xtravaganza, is a high fashion model, actress, painter, event producer, legendary ballroom personality and transgender activist. She appeared recently in *Vogue* and *Vanity Fair* as part of the groundbreaking Barney's campaign, which featured transgender models. As a result of her participation in the campaign, she was also profiled on Japanese Public TV. Over the course of her modeling career, she has worked with Academy Award-nominated costume and fashion designer Patricia Field, along with many leading fashion photographers, including Patrick Demarchelier, Terry Richardson, Danielle Levitt, and Bruce Weber. In addition to *Vogue* and *Vanity Fair,* she has appeared in national magazines, such as *Interview, Out, Amelie G, Flaunt,* and *C★ndy*. In fact, Gisele is on the gatefold cover of the Winter 2014-2015 issue of *C★ndy*, their 5th anniversary issue. Her runway work includes The Blonds, Vidal Sassoon, Nico and Adrian. Gisele is also featured in the Icona Pop video *All Night,* which has gotten millions of YouTube views. And she appeared with them at Radio City Music Hall for the 2013 finale of America's Got Talent.

Gisele also appeared in the film, *The Extra Man,* with Kevin Kline, Katie Holmes and Paul Dano and was featured in the documentary, *Lost in the Crowd* by Susi Graf.

———————

JOE: Hi, Gisele. It's great to speak with you today.

GISELE: Well, thank you. It's great to speak with you too.

JOE: You have had a long, successful career as a high fashion model, and you're one of the very few transgender women who have been able to do that. It's extraordinary because we know that it's very challenging to be transgender and to have success as a model. How have you been able to do that?

GISELE: Well, I've been able to do that by being true to myself and just following what I believe I can do and whatever I want to do—always having a very strong personality and being very professional, very respectful. I've also had a lot of people approach me to be part of this business.

JOE: People approached you because you're beautiful. But you still had to overcome the fact that you're transgender. You told me in a previous conversation that there were even some people in the industry who advised you not to disclose that you're transgender. But you've been very open and up front about that.

GISELE: Yes. They used to tell me not to tell people. But when people approached me in the street, most of the time they would not know that I was transgender. They would ask me if I was a model. And I would say no. Then I would tell them immediately that I was transgender, because I always wanted to keep it very real with whoever was approaching me. Actually, at the time, I never thought that I could be a model—that it was even possible for me because I was transgender. I had never heard of a transgender model at that time. This was around the year 1999 or 2000. People used to ask me if I had modeled. And I'd say no. One day I was approached in the West Village by a modeling agent. She asked me if I was a model. And I said no. Then she said, well, would you like to be a model? Would you like to shoot with me? I'm an agent. I represent models. And I said, well, sure. I told her immediately you have to understand one thing. I'm transgender. And she was very surprised and shocked. But then she looked at me and said, you know what? I'll still test you. We'll still shoot you. And I went and I shot. And I don't know. It was like she just gave me the opportunity to experience that. I never did before. And it was beautiful. It was great. I really loved the pictures, and I was amazed by the experience. Ever since then I believed that I could do it.

JOE: And you have done it. You've taken such great advantage of that opportunity. And there has been progress despite the fact there are lots of challenges. That progress is reflected in the Barney's "Friends and Family" campaign, which featured you and other transgender models with their family members and friends. There's a shot, for example, of you with your mother and your cousin. What would you say is the message that the campaign was communicating about transgender people by focusing on the theme of friends and family?

GISELE: Well, I think the message was that transgender people are real people. We have mothers. We have fathers. We have sisters. We have brothers. We have families. We have somewhere that we came from. So it's not like we're just these outcasts who are completely out of society. I think it was a very important campaign. It was an amazing campaign. It's a milestone in transgender history.

JOE: Building on the idea that transgender people are human beings who have relationships just like everybody else, I think that's also suggested in the current issue of C★ndy where you're on the cover with a lot of amazing transgender models and personalities, including Janet Mock, Laverne Cox, who was, of course, also on the cover of *Time* magazine, Carman Carrera, who is also participating in The Human Agenda project and Nina Poon, who photographed you for the covers of two of my books. The theme of the C★ndy issue is "Role Models"—that you and the other transgender women are role models who represent achievement and success and beauty and that you represent something positive to the community.

GISELE: Well, it's amazing that they would consider me—and us—as role models. I think that's a great honor. I don't personally consider myself to be a role model. I consider myself to be just me. I do what I feel is right and whatever I love. And I stand up for myself. I am who I want to be and who I am. So if that's being a role model, then I love it.

JOE: Well, that's something to admire. And I think that is one of the reasons you've been so successful. You are yourself. You're real. You're true to yourself. And when you stand up for yourself, you are really standing up for all people. Right? The most radical thing you can do is to be yourself.

GISELE: Yeah.

JOE: Now, in addition to your work as a model, you are also a legendary ballroom personality. You're known as the Mother of the House of Xtravaganza. Could you talk a little bit about that too? Like, what did it mean growing up as a young transgender woman to be part of the ballroom scene and a member of the House of Xtravaganza and ultimately the Mother of the House of Xtravaganza?

GISELE: Well, it meant a lot to me because it was a very artistic world that I came into, and it was like a family. I always had support from my family. But to find a group of people who support each other and who don't judge each other for our gender and who actually praise who we are—that was amazing. And being the mother is a very weird and wonderful experience, because you get to deal with so many great people. The ballroom scene has also given me a little bit more confidence about being myself and being transgender. It was about celebrating that I am transgender, and that's something that I've always admired about the ballroom scene. Because society really doesn't treat us with respect of any kind. So the ballroom movement is very important because it's saying, listen, we're here, and we're people.

JOE: As you're saying, in addition to the respect, there's celebration in the ballroom scene, the celebration of who you are.

GISELE: Yes, there's celebration. There's glamor. There's dancing. There's art. And there are a lot of major celebrities who have been influenced by the ballroom scene, such as Madonna. I mean, the ballroom scene has influenced the entire fashion industry and the entire music world.

JOE: You recently attended a ball, and you said Rihanna was there. And, of course, the House of Xtravaganza has been closely associated with Madonna and voguing. So, the ballroom scene is a trend-setting phenomenon too. And it's all about beauty and theatricality. But for you I know that it means even more than that. You've produced your own balls—the Dream Ball and the Universal Ball. I had the privilege of working with you on the Universal Ball. And I know your vision for that, which you described in an article you wrote for the *Huffington Post*. In that piece you said that you "wanted to expand the appeal and reach of the ball to include every kind of person: gay, transgender, straight, rich, poor and everything in between." You said, "I want to include people from the worlds of fashion, music, entertainment, art and the club scene." Could you expand a little bit on that message? Because that's a very big message and vision all about diversity and inclusion.

GISELE: I came up with the idea of the Dream Ball because it would be a dream for me to see everybody getting together and just enjoying themselves and not judging each other. Just celebrating beauty and fashion and dance and art. That's something that I always wanted to do. And I wanted to do it in an opulent way. To show the opulent side of all of this and a glamorous side. But also I didn't want it to be just for rich people. I didn't want it to be just for gay people or for trans people. I wanted it to be for everybody. I wanted everybody to join in this event because of the beauty that I was going to create through it. So that was my message. I wanted the ball to look like a dream. And I named the second ball the Universal Ball for the same reasons. I wanted everybody to come and enjoy it because I think it is very important that everybody just accept each other regardless of color, religion and whatever people may believe. I think it's really, really barbaric not to believe that. It's totalitarian.

JOE: The only way to come together really is to come in diversity and celebrate all of our differences, right—not to be just one thing.

GISELE: That's what makes everything beautiful. Diversity.

JOE: Not everybody celebrates that, as you said. And we're talking about the beauty that's been part of your life. And you are so beautiful. But there's a lot of ugliness out there too.

GISELE: Yes.

JOE: It must have been very difficult for you growing up as a transgender teenager in Harlem. Transgender kids are subjected to all kinds of harassment in their neighborhood by their neighbors, by the police. And it continues today. Islan Nettles was killed just a few blocks from where you grew up and where your mother still lives. And your friend Lorena

Xtravaganza was murdered in her apartment. Nobody's been brought to justice in either case. I know again from our previous conversations that you have been subjected to harassment in your own life. Could you talk a little bit about that? What was it like growing up as a transgender teenager?

GISELE: Well, growing up as a transgender teenager was difficult in my neighborhood because everyone basically had known me as a child. Ironically, at the same time, a lot of people protected me for the same reason—they had known me as a child. But once those people started moving out of the neighborhood, it was like harassment every single day. And it would be mostly because I was with a boyfriend of mine or friends of mine. And then they would to try to embarrass me. And that was very traumatizing for me. They even used to insult me when I was with my mother. When it happened, it was extremely depressing. So I had to grow up and deal with a lot of prejudice and a lot of abuse. And I just never understood why. I used to look at people and think why can't people just let people live? Why can't people just let people be? This is absurd. I mean, drug dealers would preach to me the word of *The Bible*. I used to be like, excuse me? You don't even know what you're talking about. You're pulling out one verse. How about the verses that condemn you? I just never understood why people had so much hate in their hearts, because I wasn't born, I wasn't raised, with that mentality. And it really was not a good feeling. But I overcame it because I had the support of my family. And I had the support of my friends. And that's a very important thing to have if you're going through something traumatic.

JOE: It's fundamental to have that support when you are subjected to harassment and abuse on a daily basis. And, unfortunately, as you are suggesting, a lot of people base their bigotry and their prejudice on religion. I think that was why you agreed to appear on the cover of my two religious satires. You're the innocent and angelic nun on the cover of *You Got to Be Kidding*, my satire of *The Bible*. And you're the demonic and possessed transgender pope on the cover of *Papal Bull*, which is my satire of the Catholic Church. You participated in both projects because you have such strong feelings about the fact that a lot of people use religion to justify their bigotry against gay and transgender people. And you just mentioned that you encountered that even coming out of the mouths of drug dealers in the neighborhood you grew up in.

GISELE: Exactly. I wanted to be on the cover of your books because I felt very strongly about the message that you were communicating. Religion is a major factor in a lot of the prejudice directed at gay and transgender people. It used to really get me upset when people preached the word of God and said that we were the sinners. That infuriated me. Actually when I was younger, I wanted to become a Benedictine monk.

JOE: You were attracted to religion.

GISELE: I'm still attracted to religion. Religion is mystical. It captures the spirit of so many people. It is so powerful. At the same time, it also has a horrific history.

JOE: Importantly, though, you've had support. That was also highlighted in Susi Graf's documentary, *Lost in the Crowd*, in which you are featured. Actually the support of your family is a significant message of that film. The film dramatizes the fact that when gay and transgender youth are rejected by their families, they often end up homeless and may turn to drugs and sex work. In some cases tragically these young people do not survive. So clearly without support, life can be extraordinarily difficult, even life threatening.

GISELE: Yes, and if you have support, it's still difficult. But support makes it a lot better. My advice for people who don't have support at home and who live in a community that is harmful and judgmental is to find support somewhere. Go to a center. Go where there are people like you who will support you.

JOE: Find people you have something in common with, and you can support each other.

GISELE: Find people you have something in common with who support each other and who are there for each other. There are people that are like you. There are many.

JOE: You have many different talents. For example, you're an incredible painter. You have a really powerful dark vision of reality that you capture in your painting. Sometimes it comes through in a nightmarish portrait or using nightmarish imagery. Can you speak a bit about what your painting means to you? And what are some of the themes and ideas that you are expressing through your paintings?

GISELE: Well, I'm very attracted to dark paintings and dark things because of the fact that I feel that the world is dark, and I feel that I've been through a lot of dark things in my life. I'm not the person to make bright or cheery art or an art that doesn't relate to me. This is why I'm attracted to it. I actually go on whatever is me. And I feel like I don't even try to be dark. It just happens to come out dark. I always try to put light in it. And it's like I don't like that. And it always ends up being dark. So actually I do want to do light things. But they still are dark. I guess that's just me, and it's a natural thing.

JOE: Well, I love your painting. It's dark. It's beautiful, and it's very powerful. Earlier in this conversation we talked about the idea of being a role model, the theme of the C★ndy issue. I know you don't think of yourself as a role model. But, as we've been discussing, you've had incredible experiences, and you've achieved a lot of success. What would you say to young transgender women are the important values and ideals to have to stay strong and positive?

GISELE: Well, my advice to transgender girls my whole life has been to be truthful. Be honest. Be professional. Be strong. Do what you feel is right for you with reality in mind. Always, always stay true to yourself. And no matter what anyone tells you, if it's a hundred people telling you that you can't do something, don't believe them. You can do whatever you want as long as it's a positive thing. If it's your dream, go for it.

JOE: That's a great message. It's a message that I think we all need to take to heart. Thank you so much, Gisele, for spending this time with me. It's been amazing having the opportunity to talk to you about your life.

GISELE: Thank you, Joe.

ELEGANCE **BRATTON**

"There is such a massive gap in understanding between what has been sold as the gay life and what has been the experience of gay people of color who are also being oppressed because of the color of their skin and more than likely because of their class. There's this huge gap between the mainstream gay rights movement and its ability to speak to that experience within the rainbow."

Elegance Bratton is the director of *Pier Kids: The Life,* a film about homeless LGBTQ kids of color. *Pier Kids* follows the stories of three homeless young people: DeSean, Casper and Krystal. Their stories are unique and compelling, while also representing the experiences, unfortunately, of thousands of other homeless and transient LBGTQ kids. The film also reflects Elegance's own story. At the age of 16 he left home when his family rejected him for coming out as gay. He spent the next ten years at times homeless, at other times in various temporary housing situations. He transformed his life at the age of 26, however, by joining the Marines, where he developed his skills as a photographer and a videographer. In 2014 he graduated from Columbia University.

———————

JOE: Elegance, it's a pleasure to speak with you. Your personal story is very much related to the stories of the LGBTQ kids that you tell in *Pier Kids*. I was wondering if you could begin by sharing a little of that story, because it does relate, I think, to the experience of so many people. Could you talk about what your family's reaction was, specifically your mother's reaction, when you came out as gay?

ELEGANCE: Sure. One of the primary reasons I'm making this film is to expand our notion of what it means to come out. To be clear, I never once uttered the words to my mom, "Mom, I'm gay." My mother never said to me, "If you're gay, you can't live here." I grew up in a house where my sexuality was assumed from a very young age. Like, I knew what it was. My family knew what it was, but we never talked about it. Then at the age of 16, I got into a pretty heated argument with my mom because I was missing a bunch of days from school. They called home, and said, "Something's wrong with your son. When he shows up, he's distracted, if he shows up." She confronted me. Basically at that age I was coming into sexual maturity, and I was thinking back to some childhood sexual abuse that I had been through. It caused a sort of breakdown for me, and I told her, "Hey, Mom. I was sexually abused, and that's why I'm not going to school, and that's why I'm so all over the place because I'm thinking about that and I don't know what to do about those thoughts." She responded by smacking me across the face and asking me if I was some sort of faggot. I responded by grabbing my backpack. I had twenty bucks on me, and I grew up in New Jersey. So I knew that if you didn't have anywhere to go, and you didn't really have a lot of money, you could just get a train ticket to New York, and you could walk around and distract yourself. I needed to get out of the house, so I went to the train and got on the Northeast Corridor Line. When I got on the train,

I saw what I assumed to be three black gay men. I followed them because they were having a good time. They were dancing, reading each other, making jokes. They just seemed to be really happy. It seemed like they had somewhere to go together. So I followed them, and they led me to Christopher Street for the first time. There's this great theologian, John O'Donohue, who talked about the idea of what home is. To him, home is the place where you're the most completely understood. When I arrived at Christopher Street and I saw all of these black gay men and boys and trans women and trans girls, it was crazy. It was like everybody was excited to see me, had been seemingly waiting for me to show up, and they didn't even know my name. From that point forward, from 16 on, my mom's house became one of many places that I would rest my head at night. That first night was the first time I stayed out all night, the first time I ever got a kiss from a boy, the first time I ever flirted with a boy in public, all those things. I didn't know it at 16, but that night laid the bedrock for behavioral patterns that eventually led to me leaving my mother's house for good when I was 19. From that point on, I didn't speak to her again until I joined the Marine Corp.

JOE: One question I have, though, is would you say that your experience when you first left your mother's home was sort of like a search for another family, because it seems that you did find a community? It also seems that the film is really about family. You have your biological family, and you find it untenable to live with them, and you go in search of other family-like relationships.

ELEGANCE: Yeah. I can look back on it now and say, "Yes, that's what I was looking for. I was looking for a new family." But at the time I didn't know that's what I was looking for. I didn't know that I would find that. I didn't know that was even possible. I grew up in a very homophobic household where we didn't even imagine what gay people's lives were like. We didn't think, oh, these people have jobs, and these people have relationships, and these people have houses, and they have friendships, and they have places they go to drink and listen to music. They have a whole gay culture. This was totally foreign to me when I first went to Christopher Street. But I knew intuitively that I was drawn to it. It was almost a calling in a way. So when I got there, I was pleasantly surprised to find all of these people who were excited to see me. They just seemed excited to have another person like them in the world. It was the first time that anybody was excited about me being gay.

JOE: So you had a very warm reception, and you found a community of people who undoubtedly provided you with some support. But I think it's hard for most people to imagine a person surviving on the street, even if you're not technically homeless most of the time, moving from one place to another. It just seems almost impossible to hold your life together under those circumstances, so I'm just wondering, how were you able to live without a fixed home for such a long time?

ELEGANCE: Well, that first night I didn't know. I consider that first night to be the first night I was homeless, right, because everything that I ended up doing that night, from what am I gonna eat? Where am I gonna sleep? How am I gonna wash myself in the morning? All of that happened that first night. It helped that I was young and that I was attractive. There are so many things written about gay life in the city. A lot of it has this negative connotation of the predatory element of things. That's not true. But if you're young, attractive, male and black on Christopher Street, you're going to find somewhere to sleep. You're going to find someone who wants a beautiful black boy around them. So the first thing that I did to survive was to have sex. And not in the sense of sex for money, but in the sense of sex for housing. Sex for, oh, let's go on a date, and I'll get something to eat out of it.

JOE: And, of course, your experiences living on the street inform the point of view of *Pier Kids*.

ELEGANCE: Yes. *Pier Kids* is about radically transforming the public's imagination, particularly the black community's imagination, of what a homeless person looks like and how they live. The kids in my film, myself when I was in their situation, they dress in the trendiest clothes. They know the latest music. They have the latest technology in their pocket. They don't look like homeless people. And on top of that, I would say that the word that I would think is more accurate, is the word "unhoused." I'm not eating out of a trashcan every day, but I don't necessarily have anywhere to lay my head. So when you ask how did I survive—one of the things that helped me was the fact that I went to all white schools growing up. I went to All Saints Regional when I was in grammar school in Phillipsburg, New Jersey. And I went to Seton Hall Preparatory School in West Orange for high school. So what does that mean? That means that when I'm on the pier and I'm talking to people, I have the cultural capital to be able to talk to the white punk rockers and to the white kids who are hipsters and into indie rock and things of that nature. I have certain basic cultural commonalities with them because of my upbringing. So that meant that I basically lived like a bohemian. I wrote poetry, and I ended up going to New Brunswick, New Jersey, a college town. And when you're in a college town, all these kids are plugging through the liberal arts idea of what an education is, so they're kind of primed for an individual like me. They're reading about the Beat Generation, and they're reading about Rimbaud and Jean Genet. So here I am this street kid, this street poet kid.

So there's a certain kind of cultural cache that I was able to take advantage of, so now I'm couch crashing with a bunch of middle class kids from Pompton Plains, New Jersey. I met them on the pier one night, and they're like, "Hey, we're going to a club." I'm always out at the clubs anyway, so I've always got free entry to the clubs, so I can invite them. I can say, "Hey, why don't you come to the Limelight with me. My friend's throwing a party." The next thing you know we're all partying all night till it's time to go somewhere and crash, and then I'm crashing with them. You wake up in the morning, and they still want to have a good time. And I still know where to take them. So for years that's how it was for me. And then I got older. I turned 24, 25. And all of a sudden, I'm not this cool black kid anymore. I'm the homeless black man on your couch. And all of those things that we do to homeless black people started being done to me. All of a sudden, it was, we can't have you. My parents don't want you here. Oh, I've got a girlfriend. I've got a boyfriend, all those types of things. Once I lost out on the places to crash at, I lost out on my ability to shower regularly, to shave regularly. I didn't have money for a haircut. So all of a sudden now you're trying to get a job, and you smell funny, and your hair looks crazy, and I ended up in a shelter. And I called my mom and said, "Mom, can I come home?" And she said to me, "Are you still gay?" Silence. And she suggested I join the military.

JOE: So at that point, did you feel that you had come to the end of being able to sustain that kind of transient life?

ELEGANCE: Once I got to the shelter, I saw that homelessness is a central black issue. In every shelter I've been to, the majority of the men are black. And I'm there as a 25 year old, and I'm looking at these black men—they're 50, 60 years old—they've been doing this their whole adult lives. And I realized that was going to be me, that I was them, that I'm just really getting started, although it had been almost ten years, almost ten years of my youth. The real thing is coming where I'm a grown assed man and I'm living this way, and I was just like, "I can't do this." You're in a shelter. It's horrific. There are people who have been totally washed away from society, and they know that. They feel it. The energy is just incredibly depressing. People are shooting up drugs, smoking crack, getting into fights, mumbling to themselves in the corner. And that's the only place I can sleep. So when I called my mom, I called her out of absolute desperation. I hadn't spoken to her for years at that point. And I was just like, "Look I don't want to do this. I need help." I knew inside of me that this was not meant for me, that this was not supposed to be my life. And my mom said, "Join the military," and at the time this was 2005, so Katrina had just happened, and Kanye's like "George Bush doesn't like black people," and I believed Kanye. I took that to heart. I thought he was telling the truth. So when my mom said, "Join the military," I'm like, "You must be crazy. I'm not gonna go and fight some war to kill other poor brown people behind some bullshit that I don't even believe in." And then I went back to the shelter, and they served us their stew, which I believe was Alpo. I'm almost certain it was Alpo. And I woke up the next day, and I was like, "I need to do something radically different, so I don't end up being stuck in this cycle that all these other black men are stuck in." So I left the shelter. I saw this really good-looking Marine. He had on his dress blue recruiting uniform, Sgt. Rodriguez, and it was almost like *kismet*. He looked at me. I looked at him. He crossed the street. He was like, "Hey, do you want to join the Marine Corp?" And I was like, "If I can look half as good in that uniform as you look in it, I'll do it." Two weeks later I was in Paris Island.

JOE: That changed your life dramatically, of course. Don't Ask Don't Tell was still in effect, so as you describe the experience on your website, you had to lead a double life at the same time that the Marines gave you the opportunity to develop new skills in photography and videography, and so you were really able to completely re-invent yourself.

ELEGANCE: Yes. To be honest with you, Don't Ask Don't Tell was the environment that I grew up in, that was my household environment. There are many men who are in the closet at home and out of the closet when they're not home. Everyone in the house knows that Uncle Jose has never had a wife, has never had a kid. You know what I'm saying? But for whatever reason it's a passively known secret. No one is gonna raise their hand and say, "Hey, I'm gay" or "you're gay." Because once that happens, we all know that this family falls apart.

JOE: It's an unspoken fact, but it's never acknowledged.

ELEGANCE: So that's how I grew up. By the time I got to the Don't Ask Don't Tell military, this was what I knew how to do. I knew how to conceal myself. I mean I had girlfriends. Not really, beards are more like it. But I definitely made sure that I had enough women around me. Most of my time making films for the military I spent in Thailand. Over there, a lot of the soldiers use their money to go to bars and pick up girls. So what I would do is, I would take my little 3200 bot. I would go with the other Marines to the strip bars and the red light district. I'd find a girl, and we would have a cute conversation about something, and I would get a room at a hotel and literally order room service, give them the money, and we'd just sit there and talk. Because it was important that these other men that I was working with see that a woman went into my room. What happened in that room, that's private.

But they're going to assume that all these things happened. And I would get by just like when I was in high school. I'd give a girl my number and say call me at this time because my mom's going to be home. In the military I knew what the consequences were for being found out. Outside the military, there is this idea that once you come out, things get better. I don't think that's necessarily true, I know for me and the people in my film, it wasn't 100% true. Actually coming out caused the greatest catastrophe of my life. By the time I got to the military I'd already lived through ten years of a catastrophe, so I wasn't about to put myself in an even worse position and get kicked out of that. In many ways, the Marine Corp. was a way for me to amend many of the mistakes that I'd made. At that time in my life I believed one of the mistakes I'd made was not doing a passable representation of heterosexuality to my family and my blood relatives. So when I got to the military, I was very focused on making sure that the willing suspension of disbelief was all around me.

JOE: Your experience really highlights the dangers of coming out. Within the community there is a great deal of focus on the importance of coming out. As part of this project, I had a conversation with LGBTQ activist, Ash Beckham, about this, and she also emphasized how you can't be judgmental with regard to whether or not people come out and when they come out, because the results have a dramatic effect on your life and can even be catastrophic.

ELEGANCE: Yeah. I remember when I told my mom I wanted to be a dancer. I was obsessed with Madonna. And she caught me voguing one day, and she pummeled me, man. She beat me. It was like boot camp. I remember my first time on the quarterdeck, which is like the physical punishment element of boot camp, where they're like, "All right. Get up here. Do 500 push ups. Now run in place." That kind of thing. And that's what my mom did to me when she found me voguing and I told her I wanted to be a dancer. She was like, "Do push ups. This is what men do." It was all bracketed with violence. This is what my childhood looked like, particularly around gender nonconforming behavior. You're not acting the way that a black man is supposed to act. So I'm going to correct this behavior with violence. So by the time I'm 16 and the question of coming out is brought up, how am I supposed to effectively apply any of this post-Stonewall gay rights strategy as a teenager. And how am I supposed to explain that to a parent who, because of her race, because of her gender and because of her class has been ignored by the very same movement. I think that the gay rights movement during my childhood was more concerned with expressing some aspect of queer life to middle class whites. They were not interested in expressing that to working class and poor people of color. That's why I'm making my film, to fill that gap.

JOE: Do you feel that in making the film about DeSean, Casper and Krystal, you are sort of telling your own story through their stories?

ELEGANCE: Yeah. The film essentially is a very long, drawn-out way for me to officially come out to my mother. To me, coming out is a lot more than who I sleep with. Coming out is about the totality of my experience in those ten years. Essentially what my mother would have wanted is what the military wanted from me. She would have been fine if I'd married a girl, had some kids, and if my wife came to her in the middle of the night saying, "He hasn't been home again. What's going on? Was he like this?" my mother would have been just fine with that. That conversation would have been swept under the rug. In many ways she got what she wanted. She did not want to be aware that I was leading a homosexual life. So when I say I'm coming out to my mom through this film, it is about filling in the gaps. That's very important to me, and I think for other queer people of color. There is such a massive gap in understanding between what has been sold as the gay life and what has been the experience of gay people of color who are also being oppressed because of the color of their skin and more than likely because of their class. There's this huge gap between the mainstream gay rights movement and its ability to speak to that experience within the rainbow. So it's very important to me to use the film as a way of speaking to my mom but also as a tool for working class and poor families of color to better understand their queer children and really to stimulate conversations that are difficult to have. When you watch Krystal meet her mother for the first time as a trans woman—mind you, her mother kicked her out of the house because she thought she was a black gay man—the whole conversation is in the film, and it's about, So what do I call you now? And could you wear something a little more mannish because I don't want to see you as a woman. But I can't do that, Ma, I'm on hormones now. Things in my body have changed. These types of conversations are just so difficult to have because of centuries of shame that have been piled onto bodies of color, particularly black bodies of color and around our sexuality.

JOE: Can you talk a little bit about the point of view of your film?

ELEGANCE: Let's be clear. This is entertainment. I don't even refer to my film as a documentary. I call it an experiential nonfiction film. The goal of the project, what I would like the viewer to be for the 90 minutes that they watch the film, is a Pier Kid. You are placed within my point of view. In many ways the production of it mimics how I lived. So I'm at Columbia, and I schedule my classes Monday through Thursday so that from Thursday night through Sunday morning I'm able to be homeless again. Another way of thinking about it is that the camera is a Pier Kid. We leave 116th Street for Christopher Street on Thursday, and we don't know where we're going to go for the next several days. All we know is the cast. We know Krystal. We know DeSean, and they've been cool with us, so we're gonna follow them. We're gonna hang out with them and see where they lead us to. And through Krystal I discover the ballroom thing, where the family can be remade in the house ballroom scene. Through DeSean, I discover that you can be a leader in a really difficult life situation and also the integrity of the idea of using crime to survive. In the case of Casper, he died not even a year into filming. So I only had two interviews with him. He was killed in a double hit and run on Eastern Parkway at 2:00 in the morning. He was going to visit his trans girlfriend. And what Casper teaches us is that when you have to live your life outside, you are exposed to that much more danger. It's not just about the gay bashing and police profiling, although that's very much a part of the narrative. But it's also about the laws of probability. If the relationship I have demands the nighttime in order for it to flourish, then that means that I might be skateboarding across Eastern Parkway at two in the morning with the little bit of clothes that I have, which are dark, and I could get hit by two random cars.

JOE: You're vulnerable in so many ways, because you're out at night. You're alone, and anything can happen.

ELEGANCE: Yes. So I do see educational value in what I'm doing. But my main interest is in portraying the experience of living it—making that palpable to our viewers, because I believe that's the only way that these black families will truly understand what they are pushing their children into when they make it so uncomfortable for them to be queer in their own houses.

JOE: Do you have a target date for completing the film?

ELEGANCE: Yes, it will be complete in February 2015.

JOE: Great. I understand that you're rolling out the film first into black and Latino communities?

ELEGANCE: Yeah. My favorite place to watch a black movie is in a black neighborhood like Harlem because people talk back to the screen. It kind of feels like almost a concert event in a way. I want to be able to reproduce that experience with *Pier Kids*. So what we're looking to do is to create a film experience that's somewhere between going to a ball and watching a movie. We want to be able to make this environment where communication with what's on screen and with the person next to you is fostered.

JOE: Well, I wish you great success with the film. It's so important to tell the story of homeless LGBTQ kids, transient kids, the relationship they have with their families and how they survive through making new connections and in a sense forming new families and new relationships. So, thank you so much again, Elegance.

ELEGANCE: Thank you. I appreciate it.

KEVIN FISHER-PAULSON

"Don't question what your gift is. Just give it."

Kevin Fisher-Paulson has been active in the gay movement since his college days, first at the University of Michigan and then at Notre Dame. When Kevin moved to New York after college, he worked on the first national AIDS switchboard. He was also active in a citizen patrol group called the Pink Panthers to help protect the gay and lesbian community in the city. After moving to San Francisco, he became involved in gay politics and serves as Captain of the Honor Guard for the San Francisco Sheriff's Department. He contributes regularly as a writer to *The Sentinel,* and his stories and poems have been published in *the James White Literary Review, Amethyst, Oberon, RFD* and *Suburban Wilderness.* His plays and monologues have been produced in the ODC Summerfest, Theater Rhinoceros, and the National AIDS Theater Festival. He is also the author of an incredible memoir, *A Song For Lost Angels,* which tells the story of how he and his husband Brian became the foster parents of triplets, Vivienne, Joshua and Kyle. They were born premature and had serious medical issues. Kevin and Brian nursed them back to health, loved them, but then lost the children as a result of the intervention of some anti-gay social workers and a subsequent court decision. So *A Song for Lost Angels* is on the one hand a really inspiring story, but it's also very disturbing. Fortunately, Kevin and Brian were subsequently able to adopt two other boys, Zane and Aidan, and Kevin, Brian and the boys are now living together as a family, and that is a happy ending, indeed.

JOE: Kevin, you share an amazing story in *A Song for Lost Angels*. I'm so glad that I can talk to you about this today and understand a little bit better your experience and Brian's experience as foster parents and as parents now to your two boys, Zane and Aidan.

KEVIN: Well, thank you. I'm happy for the opportunity to talk with you as well.

JOE: The first thing I wanted to ask you about was a moment that you describe in your book. You're sitting at your favorite Chinese restaurant, Yet Wah's, with Brian, and you have kind of an epiphany, a moment when you realize that you want children, and it seemed to me that it was a quintessential example of a moment of transformation, a moment of change that just sort of happens but must have a really big back story to it. So I was wondering if you could just explain how that moment happened.

KEVIN: Well, with any moment of epiphany in our lives, with any moment of great realization, we realize that that moment of change occurred because we had already begun to build the change in ourselves. Brian and I had for years been taking care of a friend, Tim, who had AIDS. He'd lived with us for several years and was then in the terminal stages of AIDS. So we had gotten into the habit of caretaking—taking in rescue dogs and really providing help for people who needed it. Also, we had gotten into the habit of creating family. Tim was very much family to us. As if by law, as if by blood, Tim was a member of our family in all ways. That night, sitting in the Chinese restaurant when I got a fortune cookie that said, "Your children respect your wisdom," I realized that that's what the build-up had been, that all along for all the years we'd been together we had been building a family, and we wanted now to reach to the next generation. We wanted to be able to share our wisdom and our love for children and the hope to create a better life for them. So, yeah, it was like suddenly in that moment that I realized it, but now looking back on it years later, I realize that we'd been building towards it all along.

JOE: So there was preparation for the moment, of course, but when you shared the idea of wanting to start a family with Brian, did you have any concerns that it would be a real surprise to him and that maybe he wasn't on the same page as you at that point with starting a family?

KEVIN: Well, one of the great things about my relationship with Brian is that it's really a relationship. We've prided ourselves on always being different. We've been together now for 28 years, and when people ask what is the secret of your happy marriage, I say actually if there's anything it's that we've learned how to disagree with each other. What's really important is to learn how to have a different opinion and still respect each other. So Brian and I—we're not the same. I'm a deputy sheriff, and he's a dancer. It's a classic Western romance—the dance hall girl and the deputy. Brian had lived a life touring where going out into the world was important to him, and I'd lived a life where building up the home was important to me. So I knew he might not agree with me on the issue. But I wanted to take the chance. We have always been the kind of people who could take chances with each other, and I think that was important. I mean, if it doesn't involve some risk, then why bother doing it? So I knew he was touring, and I knew he'd have some reservations, but I wanted to do it. Looking back on it, I think I probably would've continued pursuing a conversation with him about it if he needed more time to decide. But it was great that he realized immediately, yes, this is what we were born to do. So I got lucky that for once our opinion was the same on an issue.

JOE: But it was really a lot to take on. I mean having one child is a big challenge. You became the foster parents of triplets. They were premature. They had serious medical issues, having been exposed to drugs in the womb. One of the children, Kyle, was even in danger of dying. I believe he had a punctured intestine and a heart condition.

KEVIN: A heart valve problem, yes.

JOE: And that's just an incredible amount of responsibility to take on.

KEVIN: Yes, and did I mention that at the same time we were taking care of a dog with a failing kidney?

JOE: Oh, no!

KEVIN: And Tim was actually still alive at the time.

JOE: Yes.

KEVIN: Tim was slowly going blind and was losing weight from a severe intestinal problem. So we were balancing all those issues out. I don't want to say that we're saints. We're not. But we like to help other people. And we're both aware of what we can take on. Yeah, actually to be honest, if you were asking randomly, do you want to change a colostomy bag, I would say no, I really don't want to have to change a colostomy bag. But I realize that's what I was called to do. That was the brand of love I could give. And one of the things for me has always been, don't question what your gift is. Just give it.

JOE: Yes.

KEVIN: I'm a lousy singer. So people don't ask me to sing. But I actually turn out to be pretty funny at a party, and I turn out to be pretty good at caring for things, so people are fairly quick to ask me, hey, you know, this guy needs $100. Do you think you can find it yourself or find a way of getting it to him? I'm pretty good at finding ways of helping people. That's what my gift is, so I don't question it.

JOE: I think people around you recognized that gift because one of the things that struck me was that as challenging as this was, obviously you had a lot of support from family, friends and neighbors.

KEVIN: So one of the things is that Brian and I, in addition to discovering our ability to care, also discovered the ability to inspire, although it wasn't us inspiring people, it was those three children. People said, hey, you know, we can help these children get healthy. They said, I can knit a blanket. I can cook dinner. We had one of my friends cook dinner once a week, including sauerkraut and mushrooms, food I might not have tried on my own, and she opened me up to a lot of things, because that was the gift she could give. Her gift was being able to cook sauerkraut and mushrooms. Her gift was being able to fold the laundry on our table when we were so busy rocking and feeding and diapering the babies on the table at the same time. And so our community became a larger family. Prior to today's conversation, you and I talked about a "Human Agenda." I want to emphasize that it wasn't a bunch of gay men who got together to raise these children. It wasn't a bunch of white people who got together to watch these children. It was a bunch of people who got together.

JOE: Precisely.

KEVIN: It was friends and family that we'd accumulated over some forty years on the planet that were all excited that they could be part of the adventure.

JOE: At the same time there seemed to be problems implicit in the foster care system from the beginning. I know you had a particularly difficult time with a few of the social workers who appeared to be anti-gay, but one of the things that struck me was that there were so many different social workers you were working with.

KEVIN: We worked with over a dozen social workers up to the time we became foster parents of the triplets, and by the time we were done, we had seen over twenty social workers in our lives. And we'd seen a fair number of lawyers. The foster care system is in many ways fractured in America, and in many ways it's dysfunctional. But the important thing is this. It's an avenue for giving love. It's an avenue that, you pick up a child who needs to be loved, and you give that child your brand of love. And we've met a lot of really wonderful social workers. One of the social workers who was most committed to the family that we had put together would herself come over and heat up formula. She'd say, oh, don't worry about it. It's what we all do. We are all in this together. The social workers were just like the rest of the family who had joined us in raising the triplets. Most of them were good. Most of them were loving and generous, and most of them gave what gifts they had. And yes, in that process there were one or two social workers who had an agenda. They let the politics of their beliefs get in the way of what was really best for the children. And in the book, *A Song For Lost Angels*, I mention that one social worker was a born-again Christian who believed that gays should not have children because children can only be raised properly by a man and a woman in love. I challenged that assumption. I think any loving people can raise children, any loving people who are willing to make the commitment—because raising a child is a commitment. It means you don't go out on Saturday night anymore, and it means that you don't get to watch that TV show you've always watched, and it means that the house is a little less clean than it used to be, and it means that you have to get a bigger car. It means a lot of things. And what he didn't understand was, it is that commitment to love, which is more important than any genes or any chromosomes or any political agenda. Unfortunately he was the social worker with the most to say in the case.

JOE: Yes. He made the difference in terms of returning the children to their mother, who was clearly irresponsible, had incredible problems of her own with mental illness and also substance abuse. You mentioned the platitude that children are better off with a mother and a father. It's always stated as if it's this self-evident truth when we know all sorts of families have all kinds of problems. And to your point, the one thing that is incontrovertible is that children do best when they're loved.

KEVIN: Children certainly do best when they're loved—even that love that we gave the triplets for a year. I like to think that there was something transformational in that and that it gave them enough to go on. I've been told that Kyle, the boy with the colostomy, would not have been alive had it not been for the level of care we gave him, feeding him every two hours, changing the colostomy bag, doing the exercises, getting him the heart surgery, getting him the intestinal surgery. And I do believe that. I believe that one of the good things I've done in this life is that I kept that child alive for the first year, that most critical year of his life. I know there was a reason why I took care of Kyle. I am sad that we're not together anymore, but I hope that we gave those triplets the push that got them started in life and that we showed them early in their lives what love was all about. And I hope that's enough for a happy life for them.

JOE: Have you been able to track where they are now? I know that after they returned to the mother, she lost them again, and they were back in foster care.

KEVIN: Because we were foster parents, we had almost no rights in this situation, and that's one of the concerns about the foster care system—that the foster care parents themselves have no legal rights. So we only know by accident anything that happened to them. We did know a social worker who actually had some knowledge of the system, who was able to tell us a few years later that the mother had so badly abused them that they were taken away from her. That made me really sad. I have no animosity to the birth mother, because she couldn't help being the woman that she was. She was a person with a lot of challenges and a lot of issues. The only thing that I regret is that her family did not see where the children would be most loved. I hope wherever they are in the world that they are well loved.

JOE: But you were able as you said in the book to make the choice instead of getting stuck to move forward and to hope to make another kind of joy, and you and Brian have done that by going on to adopt two children.

KEVIN: Yes, if I could sum up the book, it would be, what do you do the day after the worst day of your life. Sad things happen to all of us. They happen to you. They happen to me. I am, if anything, lucky. I've had the worst day of my life. There is no day for me worse than the day I lost my three children. That is the absolute worst. But we have a choice in life when bad or sad things happen to us. We can either sit in that pain, or we can move on. And everybody takes a different amount of time sitting with that pain. Brian and I knew we had done a great job of parenting. We learned in that year with the triplets that gosh we can make the best bacon, and we make really good parents. We're really good at this. The children were joyful. The children were happy, and the children were well cared for. We knew that was something we did well, so to not continue giving that gift would be a shameful use of what we were. Not a day does not go by without us thinking of the triplets, but I like to think it was the mistakes we made with the triplets that led us to be better parents to Zane and Aidan, because Zane really never had to sit through my figuring out how a diaper actually works.

JOE: You were an expert by then.

KEVIN: Exactly. He never had to go through my experiment with how to get the formula to the right temperature. He got it at the right temperature on the very first round. And he got the advantage of wow! I know what it's like to lose a child, so I know I'm going to give him all of my love and cherish every single moment with him. I let him know that each moment with him was important. Not tomorrow's test or yesterday's basketball game, but this very second that we're sitting on the floor rolling the ball is the most important moment we have because we might lose it tomorrow.

JOE: You make that point in the book. It's really so important to live in the moment. As you said, we all experience tragedy and setbacks. But if we get stuck in that moment, then we deny ourselves the potential of joy in the future. Although you experienced that loss, it certainly prepared you and Brian as parents for your two sons today.

KEVIN: Because joy takes different shades, and you can't really say I want this flavor of joy when the other flavor is available. My life is immensely joyful because of Zane and Aidan. And my heart is open in so many ways that I never thought possible. They are different challenges than the triplets would have been. Both of my boys were born drug exposed, so they have severe learning challenges and a couple of behavioral challenges. But we get through that, and, like I said, I've had the worst day of my life, so if I get called to the principal's office because Zane has had a fight with somebody, really in the grand scheme of things, I can't get too upset about it. It's not worth it.

JOE: You're able to put that in perspective.

KEVIN: Yes.

JOE: Well, this is just an inspiring story. It shows people how two loving men can be parents, can be so giving, can devote their lives to children, and I think anyone with an open mind may have their mind and their heart changed by your memoir, *A Song For Lost Angels*. I recommend that everybody go out and buy it. You will be inspired. It is heartbreaking, but there is another chapter, and it's a chapter full of joy. So, Kevin, thank you so much. It's been a delight talking to you.

KEVIN: Thank you for talking with me. I greatly appreciate the opportunity.

HIDA VILORIA

"Doctors want to make sure we grow up to identify as men or women. And the truth is, even with the surgeries going on, some of us don't. And it's natural. Why would we? Right? My body is androgynous. It makes sense that my gender identity might be too."

Hida Viloria is a writer, lecturer and intersex activist. Hida's mission is to promote equality for intersex people, indeed, to promote equal rights for all people. Hida is the chairperson of OII, the Organisation Intersex International, and the director of its American affiliate. Hida writes her own blog, *Intersex and Out*, and has written about intersex issues for the *New York Times*, the *Advocate, Ms.*, the *American Journal of Bioethics*, the *Global Herald*, and CNN.com. Hida co-authored with OII-USA associate director Claudia Astorino *Brief Guidelines for Intersex Allies* and is the author of *Your Beautiful Child: Information For Parents*, which provides tips on how to talk to family and friends about your intersex newborn. Hida is also featured in the documentaries *Gendernauts, One in 2000*, and *Intersexion* and recently became the first openly intersex person to speak at the United Nations as a participant in the symposium, Sports Comes Out Against Homophobia.

JOE: It's a great pleasure to speak with you today, Hida.

HIDA: Thank you, Dr. Joe. I'm honored and thrilled to take part in this project. Such a beautiful mission!

JOE: Thank you so much, Hida. You're an amazing educator on what it means to be intersex. But I think you would agree there are still a lot of people who need to be educated. So I was wondering if you could begin by talking about what it means to be an intersex person.

HIDA: Yes, many people still don't know who we are. Part of that is because the language has changed over the years. Originally, we were known as hermaphrodites. When I use that word, people understand that it refers to being born with a certain type of body. Now "intersex" is the preferred label, in part to avoid the misunderstanding that "hermaphrodite" promotes that we're actually both male and female, which is humanly impossible.

JOE: That you would have both a penis and a vagina.

HIDA: Exactly. Or that you would have testes and ovaries and could potentially impregnate yourself. We have a mix of male and female reproductive traits, not two fully functioning sets of each. The word "hermaphrodite" is also negative for some people in the community on a personal level. It's a little bit like the word "queer." A lot of older intersex folks had the word "hermaphrodite" hurled at them in a very insulting way and in violent scenarios. So it has a bad association for some members of the community. So now we use the word "intersex." In addition to referring to people who have characteristics of both sexes, "intersex" refers to people who have atypical sexual characteristics. An example of that would be people who are born without an actual vaginal opening but otherwise look completely female. There are about thirty different types of intersex variations. So there are many ways that people can be intersex. We're not a homogenous category. You'll have intersex people who look very male and intersex people who look very female and everything in between. I think the easiest way for people to think about it is that biological sex exists on a spectrum. Most people can be described as male or female pretty easily. But there's always a gray area. How different does one's body have to be to qualify as intersex? How small would a penis have to be for a man to be considered an intersex man? Or on the flipside how large would a clitoris have to be for a woman to be considered intersex? It is actually quite subjective. One doctor might label a baby a female without issue, while another might say, no, that child has a DSD [i.e., a "disorder of sex development"]—the medical label for intersex—and we need to fix it. That alone shows you how biological sex, like orientation, is a spectrum with many shades of gray. We're kind of those shades of gray.

JOE: Most people do have a binary view of gender. They think that people are either male or female period when, in fact, some people are intersex. Actually there are many more intersex people than is generally realized. You make the point on your website that intersex people are actually about as common as red heads, constituting about 1.7 percent of the population.

HIDA: Right. Thank you for bringing that up. That research comes out of Brown University. When you take all the different variations, it's about 1.7 percent. There is a popular statistic that says one in 2,000. But that's where the genitals are so ambiguous that a team of doctors gets called in. That's the one in 2,000 figure.

JOE: You make the point, Hida, that being intersex is a variance. It's not an abnormality, which to me is such a terrible word. The words "normal" and "abnormal" suggest the tyranny of the norm. In fact, the medical profession has pathologized intersex people just as they've pathologized transgender people. I had a great conversation as part of this project with Dr. Carys Massarella, who's a transwoman physician who makes the point that there's nothing biologically hazardous about being transgender. It doesn't raise your blood pressure. It doesn't increase your cholesterol. Yet it's been pathologized through the terminology of gender identity disorder and dysphoria. And being intersex has similarly been pathologized with the term "disorders of sex development," when again, except in rare cases, there is no biological hazard to being intersex.

HIDA: Right. And that shows you the incredible strength of the prejudice against people that fall outside of our sex and gender norms. Being gay used to be a disorder. In fact, I remember when I was outed because I am also, as I used to say, a lesbian—and then as I embraced being intersex, as I now say, "queer." When he found out I was a lesbian, my father at one point said, "You have too many friends with those psychosexual disorders." And I just thought he had come up with some new creative, bigoted term, because he actually is homophobic. I didn't even realize at that time that that is actually the terminology. He was just using a label he had learned in medical school.

JOE: Yes. Terminology from the medical profession, which then precipitates a language of bigotry.

HIDA: Yes. And we haven't been as vocal and out there as the transgender community. They're doing a great job. People still think of being intersex as a medical issue. And part of that is because, OK, intersex has not been in our minds in any other way. A lot of people don't see a problem with the disorder label, because they're looking at it through this medicalized kind of lens. But that label exists for the same reasons "psychosexual disorder" existed for gays.

JOE: And it's not just that the medical profession is pathologizing being intersex. In this case, it leads to a really terrible practice. Obstetricians perform operations on newborns that basically determine whether they are boys or girls. It's a barbaric practice that is totally subjective in its application. And it changes that baby for life.

HIDA: Exactly. It's irreversible. You cannot bring those parts back. That's why I speak out about this issue. Because I'm blessed, honestly. It's almost a miracle that being born in 1968 in New York City when and where these practices were incredibly common, I did not undergo a clitoral reduction surgery. That's what would have been recommended, but my father is a physician. And he was in medical school before these barbaric practices were introduced. And, in fact, he is from Colombia, so even my older brother is intact. He wasn't circumcised. That is a U.S. practice. It's not practiced regularly throughout the rest of the world. So he wasn't even used to genital cutting in that respect either. He came from a viewpoint, a very sound one I think, that if the baby is healthy, let's not operate or cut it up. Of course, most people don't have much of a medical background. They get pressured by whatever recommendations doctors make. And many people don't get second opinions. Many people are afraid to even question their doctors. I've heard from so many parents. Honestly, it takes years of healing after they realize the mistake that they made.

JOE: There must be so much guilt.

HIDA: Yeah, many feel guilty. Totally. The one thing I will say about the surgeries is that they don't achieve the goal of helping people to fit in. I didn't have surgery, and I feel I fit in much more. And the few people I've met who did not have these types of surgeries are so well adjusted. This is what I've seen in people who are allowed to grow up as they are. We form our own healthy identity and our own healthy relationships with our bodies.

JOE: Performing a surgery is not necessarily going to create a happy, well-adjusted person. It's really support and acceptance. Of course, there's a difference—though many people don't recognize it--between birth gender and gender identity. Most people identify with their birth gender, but some don't. And the way that we experience and express gender can change over time. For example, you, Hida, identified at one point as an intersex woman. And now, if I'm correct, you simply identify as intersex.

HIDA: Exactly. So why mess with a baby when you have no idea what its future gender identity will be? Doctors have taken the position that this is obviously a defect, so we have to fix it. Well, no, it's actually not. It's a natural, healthy variation. All genitals are different, and they're all fine. As long as they're functioning and healthy, they are fine. People who have these surgeries can feel like damaged goods. I mean there's an inherent, deep, ongoing message that there's something wrong with you in a sexual way. So, all that does is make people not want to be partnered. And not want to have relationships. It creates fear of intimacy. Which is exactly what it's intended to eliminate, which is the irony. I haven't had fear of intimacy because my body's different. It hasn't been an issue. Ever, actually. But this is totally different than the people who have had surgery So, yeah, I think that's what's really important for parents to know.

JOE: I think it's important to point out too that surgery isn't required for parents to decide to raise their child as a boy or a girl. And this is precisely what OII recommends. It would clearly be difficult in today's society for a child to grow up identifying as intersex rather than male or female. Parents need to determine whether their child will be best supported and accepted by growing up as a little girl or a little boy and then act accordingly. Then that little girl or little boy can decide to be cisgender or transgender once they grow into an awareness of their gender identity without having had genital surgeries.

HIDA: Right. Or neither gender.

JOE: Yes. Precisely. Each individual can decide as they grow and mature and become aware of their gender identity. I would also make the point that if an intersex person decides to identify as intersex, you could say that they are actually cisgender, although it's a term that's used within the binary. In other words, you could decide I'm not a boy. I'm not a girl. I'm intersex. That's what I was born. That's what I am.

HIDA: Yes, and that's how I identify. The funny thing is when I first heard the term "cisgender" and saw the original definition, which was that you feel you match with your natal gender, I thought, oh, I'm cisgender. I'm a cisgender intersex person. But actually now the term "cisgender" means that you identify with the gender you were assigned at birth. So by that definition, I am no longer cisgender, since no one is assigned intersex at birth in the U.S.—or almost anywhere else. But I'm not transgender either, which according to the cisgender definition I'm supposed to be by default. I'm intersex, but the binary framework of the cisgender definition doesn't allow for my experience or existence. The medical profession engages in all this theorizing about the impossibility of having an androgynous gender identity. In support of that view, the surgeries are done not just to fix the body but to fix the ultimate adult gender and put it into the binary of man or woman. Doctors want to make sure we grow up to identify as men or women. And the truth is, even with the surgeries going on, some of us don't. And it's natural. Why would we? Right? My body is androgynous. It makes sense that my gender identity might be too.

JOE: The medical community should not be the guardians of the norm and impose this totalitarian binary view on being a male or a female. To insist that you have to identify as male or female and if you don't do it, you're not going to be happy. Why?

HIDA: Exactly. Because there can be an intersex or androgynous gender identity as well.

JOE: Here's something that really puzzles me, and there's no definitive answer. But why do you think gender is such a radioactive issue? I mean, certainly if you are, quote, "born a boy," and you decide to be a transgender woman, because that's who you really are, there is tremendous reaction to that on the part of so many people. And there's so little understanding of what it means to be intersex. But there seems to be all of this emotion and hostility attaching to gender. What is that all about?

HIDA: You know, that's an amazing, important question. One of the things that come to mind is the very deeply rooted sexism in our culture. I think there is a human tendency to create hierarchies. Class is one. Race has been one. Sex has been one and sexual orientation as well. Of course, today people can't be openly racist. People can't say they're better because they're white like they could in the olden days, right?

JOE: Yes. So people who have the need to feel superior find another outlet, targeting someone because they are different or part of a minority. They make the fact that someone is different or exceptional the basis for bigotry rather than celebration. Of course, difference and diversity are what make us great. Not many people are brilliant, so it's different to be brilliant. It's certainly different to be a genius. They're aren't many geniuses around. Should we denigrate geniuses like Mozart or Einstein and call them abnormal?

HIDA: Exactly. I love how we're on a very similar page. On one occasion, I was engaged in a kind of debate with certain physicians, and they kept using the word "abnormal" to describe intersex differences and variations. And I said, you know, your use of this word is stigmatizing. And they're like, well, but it's accurate. It's not the norm. And I said, I understand, yes, it's not the norm. And I used the same example. I said, neither is being a genius. Neither is being a musical prodigy. Neither is being extremely attractive. But we don't say about a really beautiful baby, oh, look how abnormally attractive they are.

JOE: And what about when the norm is mediocrity?

HIDA: Exactly.

JOE: So normal is not necessarily good.

HIDA: Exactly. One bit I want to add to the gender issue, which I think is unfortunate, but I see it happening now is that it's becoming more of an economic issue as well. For example, Lego toys, which I loved as a child--they were genderless, right? Maybe boys happen to like Lego more. I don't know. But now they have this whole girls line of Lego, which I find incredibly sad because the girls line has little things in it meant to kind of target girls, but I see it as really creating and reinforcing for girls what they're supposed to like. Things that are considered girlie in our culture. But what that creates economically is a new revenue source. Now Sally can't inherit her older brother's Lego kit, because, oh, that's a boy kit. Mom, I want the girl kit..

JOE: It's all about making money off of gender stereotypes.

HIDA: It's happening a lot. Sexism is strong in our culture, obviously. It infuses everything that we think about love and relationships. I think it also is at the heart of the deep emotional fear around gender. Parents are just afraid. My own mom, for example, was very loving, very caring. She passed away this past year. Her biggest fear when she found out I was a lesbian was just that I wouldn't find love. I think a lot of parents feel the same. If they have a trans child or an intersex child, they wonder how will this child find love? They think boys are supposed to be with girls. Now my boy wants to be a woman. How does this all work? It just makes people question these very deeply rooted ideas that we're raised with.

JOE: It's perfectly understandable for parents to be concerned about their children, but it's also problematic when they project their own values and beliefs onto their children.

HIDA: Exactly.

JOE: We have to allow our children to be who they are.

HIDA: Exactly. And that brings me to something I'd like to address, which I mentioned earlier, about how the intersex community hasn't been as vocal and out there as, for example, the transgender community. The vast majority of us are still in the closet. It's because of the gendercide we're undergoing. I call it "gendercide" because there is a global institutional move to eradicate intersex people. We're not killed, but our intersex traits are removed. Imagine if you took African babies and dyed them white to try to remove their blackness. Our intersexness is being removed. After undergoing this gendercide, many people are not psychologically capable of subjecting themselves to more public scrutiny. We don't have the luxury that the rest of the community has to grow up with our bodies intact. To grow up without doctors spreading our legs and peering at us, when we're young children. That's what we go through. Trans people are able to grow up intact, as different as they feel from the mainstream dynamics.

JOE: That's true. At the same time, trans people are tremendously marginalized and denigrated. It's even dangerous to walk down the street as a trans woman.

HIDA: I agree.

JOE: But you're right. Intersex people are subjected to barbaric surgeries when they're newborns, babies or children. The surgeries eradicate their intersex identity and perpetrate a form of genocide.

HIDA: It's brutal. It was finally declared to be torture by the U.N. Special Rapporteur on torture. It's been likened to sexual abuse, which it is. The psychological impact is so great that most intersex people when they reach adulthood are just trying to survive and heal their wounds and fit in so they can avoid more unwanted attention. As a result, many keep the fact that they are intersex private.

JOE: How can you celebrate yourself when you've been mutilated and subjected to an operation that's intended to obliterate your identity?

HIDA: Exactly. And that's really where we are. We have just been so damaged, so discriminated against, that it is difficult for us to stand up. But, fortunately, the more people like yourself take notice and are amazing allies and help us educate others, the easier it becomes.

JOE: You are standing up, though, Hida, and you are very courageous. That's why I'm so delighted that we were able to speak today. You're such a powerful and passionate advocate on behalf of intersex people.

HIDA: Thank you. Can I mention one thing, Joe, that we didn't touch on?

JOE: Please do.

HIDA: I do want to make one thing clear because people get confused about it. While we are physically different, we have, just like non-intersex people, the same range of sexual orientations and the same range of gender identities. The reason that we are included as the "I" in the LGBTI community is not because all of us are gay or lesbian or trans. It's that we do not conform to sex and gender norms. And that's why we get discriminated against. In fact, when we're born, it's often assumed that we might grow up to be gay. It's kind of viewed as a tip off. When people see a body that is not male or female, they assume, oh, this baby will grow up to be gay or maybe trans—let's avoid that by performing "normalizing" surgery. This is why I often say that intersex people are on the front lines when it comes to facing homophobia and transphobia. We are often more vulnerable to it than L, G, B or T folks are, despite the fact that we may not grow up to be L, G, B or T. That's important for people to understand. A lot of straight intersex people look like the sex they were assigned at birth, and they feel like it, and they're married to the opposite legal sex.

JOE: Well, there's tremendous confusion about gender identity and sexual orientation. In most cases, they have very little to do with one another. There is this association of being trans with being gay or lesbian or that there's something sexual about being transgender and all those horrible jokes about transgender women wanting to be in the women's bathroom. It's just ignorance, really. And you're making a very powerful point that intersex people are just like everybody else. They span the full spectrum of sexual orientations and gender identities. The point of this project—the reason I call it The Human Agenda—is that we're all human beings with the same goals, wanting to be happy and free. We have to stop denigrating and demonizing people on the basis of difference. We need to celebrate difference and say that the one common thing we have together is that we are human.

HIDA: Yes. I love it.

JOE: Thank you again, Hida. You've been very generous with your time. It was a great pleasure and an honor to speak with you today.

HIDA: Thank you, Dr. Joe.

IAN HARVIE

"It is brave to be yourself. Absolutely it is. I'm not perfect at it either. It has to be a daily conscious practice to do so."

Ian Harvie is a stand-up comedian. He performs across the U.S. and internationally. He is the host of the *Ian Harvie Show*, a talk show that highlights LGBTQ guests. His film, *Ian Harvie Superhero*, was released in March 2014.

JOE: I'm really excited to have the chance to speak with Ian Harvie. Ian is one of the funniest guys walking the planet right now. He uses his life experience as a trans man as the basis for a lot of his humor. Ian queers the traditionally macho world of stand-up in unbelievable ways and in the process educates people and creates understanding where there may have been none previously. Ian, great to be talking with you today!

IAN: Thanks, Dr. Joe.

JOE: Ian, you did an interview with Lucas Silveira of The Cliks, and you said something really interesting. You said that you were an identity collector, that you embrace all of your multiple identities, and that's a concept that not too many people have. Whether they're cisgender or transgender, most people think they're one personality and one character that's consistent throughout their lives. Could you share with me a little bit more of that idea because it's really kind of a revolutionary form of self-identification?

IAN: Well, why pick just one? We are so multi-dimensional. You've heard the expression of people refusing to be put in a box. I just wanna take that further and say, not only am I not in a box, but I'm not just one thing or two things or even three things, and I hope to keep evolving into many things. I've been many things, and I didn't necessarily leave one behind to take on another, and that's something that a lot of people think that you have to do. You know, when I was a kid I was a masculine kid, I was a tomboy. That's still part of me. That didn't leave me. And then as I grew older, I grew into this—this butch female body person that I didn't have a language for at the time. I knew that I was masculine, but there wasn't a word for me, and someone introduced that word "butch" to me as a possible gender, as a possible descriptor, and I was like, wow, that is me, like that really is me, and it felt really good to my ears.

JOE: As a revelation in itself right?

IAN: Yeah, it was. When you find a word or a language that identifies you, it's kind of like a kick in the stomach in a really good way. So we all walk around looking for that language. I guess some of us are complacent to be just (in fake macho accent) "Well, I'm a man. I'm good with that. What else do I need to know?" Like, I'm sure there are people out there that really don't care, and that's fine too if they don't, but I'm kind of obsessed with it.

JOE: And you continue to incorporate all of those identities.

IAN: Yeah, definitely, you know "dyke" is a word that I really love. "Dyke" really resonated with me. "Butch" resonated with me, "trans man"—all of these words. And as I go through life, I'm not giving up one identity—like I'm not trading cards here you know. I'm not giving up one for the other. I really feel like they're all a part of me and a part of my history, and it's real important for me to remember all of those things because they've gotten me to where I am now and I would never want to give up my history. So I am a collector, and as I continue to grow and expand, I am constantly looking for the next word that might feel like that is me or that it resonates or that it just feels good on my ears like, "Wow, that's really nice. I like that a lot." There was a part of me that was like I don't know if I'm male. I know I'm perceived as male, but I don't know if that's one of my words, and someone said f to x and that x is a variable that can change and can ebb and flow, and maybe x some days is butch, and maybe x some days is masculine, and maybe sometimes it is male, but it was one of those things that was like, Oh right, we are constantly changing.

JOE: And now you're a superhero, which is pretty special in itself, right?

IAN: There is some power in saying "Ian Harvie, Superhero."

JOE: I love the idea that you say it. There's power in asserting that you're a superhero, right? You project yourself into an identity, and then you just start living within that.

IAN: Yeah, I think that if anything I would be my own personal superhero—out of my own willingness to explore and not live my life by what the whole world tells me I should be.

JOE: I think the term is appropriate because one of the bravest things that anybody can do is to be themselves regardless of how anybody reacts, and if being yourself means being trans, that's a really brave thing to do.

IAN: Yes, I agree that it is brave to be yourself. Absolutely it is. I'm not perfect at it either. It has to be a daily conscious practice to do so. It's not something where you say, "OK. I'm me now. I'm all good." It really is like a daily questioning. What am I doing today? Whether it's about my transness or about being a good person every day. When I came out to my parents and I said to them that I liked girls but I was physically a girl, something happened. I was kind of cracked open and began constantly seeking expansion. And I knew that liking girls was the tip of the iceberg for me. I was also exploring my gender in lots of ways but not consciously until I met a guy like me, and then I was like, "Oh my God, that's me." I saw myself in somebody else. And since that time, there's just been this constant seeking of what's next. What else you got, Universe? What else is there? What else can I do? What else can I be? How else can I expand?" And that's something that's kind of involuntary, that once you make this huge acknowledgement about yourself, it's very deep and personal. It's almost like you can't go back to being shallow and unknowing once you've been cracked open in that way and are willing to explore gender and be vulnerable with yourself. It's like I have to constantly seek now. And I like that. I like that everything that I hear, I say, "Who says it's supposed to be like that?" And then I usually go through some version of deconstructing that, like, why do I think that? Do I believe that? And then rebuild it and see if it looked like it did before I tore it down. I don't want to live my life the way I did before, which was I lived in fear. I was afraid of what would happen to me. And so the best way to combat that fear for me is to seek and move forward. I have a friend and actually you know him—Buck Angel—he said to me, before my chest surgery and before testosterone he said, "Dude, your life is gonna change so much." At the time I thought, "Yeah, my life is gonna be amazing once I don't have a chest anymore, and once I'm on testosterone." But it just was not that simple. It was so much bigger than that, and I don't know if that was what he was referencing, but my life has changed so much because of that expansion. And outside of the physicality of my transformation, there is so much change that has gone with it.

JOE: What you're describing as constantly seeking could be, on the one hand, a very private experience, but what is fascinating to me is that it's multi-level in your case because you're doing it so publicly by being a stand-up comedian and using your life experience and your seeking as a basis for a lot of your comedy.

IAN: Personally, I think the best comedy out there is when I witness real vulnerability on stage. You don't want to be so vulnerable that the audience feels complete discomfort. But you want to sort of take them on a rollercoaster ride where you're vulnerable and then it's heartbreaking and then it's peppered with seriousness and even more peppered with laughs—I mean that's my favorite kind of comedy. And for me, I have no problem being as out as I can possibly be on stage, no problem whatsoever. I want to get up there and be vulnerable and talk about sex and gender and my body and my relationships and love and family, and that's my identity on stage right now. But everybody's got that. Every comic has their identity on stage, but my personal favorite is vulnerability. One of the very first shows where I witnessed that was the Whoopi Goldberg special back in the 1980s on HBO. Whoopi had these characters that were hilarious and heartbreaking. There was this little black girl character who put a shirt on her head and talked about how she wished that she was white. She wanted long, luxurious blonde hair. I remember how much it struck me that it was so sad that this little girl thinks that it's better to be white, and that was a very serious message, but Whoopi made it so endearing and really, really funny. And I was laughing and crying at the same time. And that's something that was so powerful to me that when I started to develop as a comic, I thought, "That's how I want to be. I want to talk about things that mean something, and I want to make people laugh about it and feel comfortable about it." It had to be a part of who I was up there in order for me to do comedy, in order for it to make sense for me to do comedy.

JOE: Well, I'm glad you mentioned that because I wanted to ask you, when you first started as a comedian, were you able to be that vulnerable and use your life experience as a trans man the way that you do now, because quite obviously there is so little understanding of what it means to be transgender, right? And if you come out there as a totally unknown stand-up, that's got to be tough, and your success is certainly going to vary with different audiences as it would anyway, but I'm just wondering, were you able to do that right out of the chute, and what was the reaction.

IAN: When I first started doing comedy, I came out as queer on stage, and that is one of my identities that I love, that I collected and that I own. And I never said "lesbian" on stage. I know people probably just assumed it. I had short hair. I was very masculine. I was like, "I know what you're thinking. What's this big old dyke going to say?" Any time I said something like that they would laugh. At the time I was out in my personal life to my friends and my family as trans. But I did not come out on stage as trans until about two years into my career, and it's funny that's when I also realized who I was on stage. The very first time I ever came out on stage, I was absolutely petrified, and the rule of thumb in comedy is if you're scared, they're scared. If you're having a good time, they're having a good time. If you're relaxed, they will laugh. And so whatever you're putting out there, you will get back. And so the very first time I was very nervous. They were very nervous. I didn't do terrible. I didn't have a meltdown, so they didn't have a meltdown, but I was nervous. And so it was visible. And what I realized was, in my personal life I'm very comfortable with who I am. I need to bring that to the stage. I need to not just be funny, but I have to show them that I'm OK. Like listen, you guys don't have to worry about me. I'm all right up here. And not just as a comic, but I'm OK with my gender. I'm OK with what's happening. I'm OK with what I'm talking about. I'm OK that you have so many questions right now. And so part of my job up there is not just to make people laugh but to also make them feel comfortable. It took me a few shows before I just basically—right before I went on—said, screw it. I know who I am. And that's not up for debate. What's interesting is that this is something LGBT people in general have to say to ourselves before we come out. We have to say, Listen I know who I am. This isn't up for debate. I don't need to get into any arguments with anybody about this. I'm going to go out there and just be me. And that would be a quiet mantra of mine before I would go on stage. And that to me was sort of my calming place, and if I could get to there before I went up on stage, then that would make it all right. And even if my jokes weren't landing, if my punch lines weren't landing, it was still OK. Being comfortable in your skin as a person no matter what you're doing is one of the greatest tools. If you have that, then I think you have everything. I'm not perfect at that still in my very private intimate life.

JOE: Nobody is.

IAN: Right, which is so great when you say that. Nobody is. It's so important that you just said that. I just want to say, what happened for me on stage was this: I thought I was the only one who ever felt the way that I did, and then I met other guys like me, but what I realized about audiences was that every single person in that audience was struggling, on some level with not being enough in relation to their gender. And that was a very powerful moment for me to realize that, know what, if being a transgender person is someone who was born biologically female or male and then later grows up into a discomfort in their body in relation to their gender, I have just described every single person on the planet. There is nobody on the planet that feels 100% OK about their bodies. There are men who are modifying their bodies to be more masculine, women to be more feminine. And I thought, "Oh my God. This is our common place. This is our shared experience." So it doesn't matter when I joke about this stuff. It's gonna be universal. Even though I'm saying I'm trans and I'm different, really I'm unifying us, because what I'm talking about is so similar across the board for everybody. And at the end of my shows, I talk about that—how we have this great shared experience and how no one feels 100% OK, and if you do, then you're the weirdo, not us, cos we're all struggling. And that's something that everybody gets a big laugh out of. And it's also something that really helped me as a comic perform better because I didn't feel like I was different. I felt like I was the same, and I think that I was having these relational moments with the audience, which is a really beautiful arc in comedy and life. It's one of the best things that I could have ever realized.

JOE: Wow! Well, you mentioned the whole idea of wanting to feel comfortable in your skin, which is certainly a common human experience. We all want to feel that way. We all struggle with our identities whether we're cis or transgender. For a lot of transgender people I think it's safe to say feeling comfortable in one's own skin has to do with passing. I'm really interested in getting your thoughts on that, because in one of your interviews you were saying that you sort of feel like you come across maybe as a gay guy when you're with your girlfriend and you're in a gay bar and other gay guys are thinking, "Oh, they feel really sorry for your girlfriend because you're gonna break her heart, and they're gonna help you do that." And it also made me think of what transgender women go through. Janet Mock said recently, "Passing is fundamental to survival." But I know beautiful transgender women, and ironically, passing can put you in great jeopardy, because if you're a beautiful transgender woman, you can get hit on anywhere by straight guys who are not comfortable with their sexuality and who would certainly not be comfortable recognizing they just hit on a woman with a penis. So I was wondering about your thoughts on passing and the ambiguities and sometimes the awkwardness involved in passing.

IAN: Well, I do think there are clearly safety issues for trans people and whether or not they pass. If you think about it, the history of quote unquote gay bashing is probably more the history of gender bashing. I think it's rare that a man on the street has gotten bashed because he loved another man. It is more commonly because someone's gender was perceived as not masculine enough or not feminine enough. So there are intense safety issues for trans people or gender variant people in general. There are straight guys who are perceived as feminine who have gotten bashed, and the same thing happens with butches who are perceived as not feminine enough. So, yes, what Janet Mock says about passing being essential for survival, with the high numbers of violence against trans women, makes sense to me. But I don't think that it is trans people's work to be more feminine or more masculine. It's really non trans people's work to stop defining realness. What that is. It is the work of people who are not trans to let go of that ideology and to say it doesn't matter. So I understand what Janet is saying, and I love her, and it is absolutely true what she is saying. But I think that realness is way overrated. I remember the first time that I passed as a guy. I was in a gas station in my hometown back in Maine. I was in a Mobile station, and I went in. I had a few chin hairs, and my facial shape had changed, and I know my shoulders had filled out in a way. I remember that moment, and I was angry about it. It was weird. It's funny cos I thought at the time that I was doing all of this to pass, to look like a guy to the rest of the world, and when it happened finally in a very real way and not as someone making a mistake because they over-looked my chest, I was angry about it. And I couldn't figure out why it bugged me that this guy just called me, "Yo, bro. OK, thanks buddy, I'll see ya later. See ya next time, buddy." But I think I was angry about the privilege that it gave me. I was kind of angry that, "Listen, I'm not one of you. I am a man, but I'm not that kind of man. I'm not one of you. Don't include me in your group. That's not what I want. That's not why I did this." I did all of this to feel better in my skin. It had nothing to do with seeking the approval of the world and how they saw me. But I also realized that I can't deflect what people see me as. I can't change their idea. All I have to do is focus on what makes me feel good in my skin, and this hap-pens to be it, and this happens to be what people see, and ac-tually what I want is to be perceived as queer. It's interesting that holding my girlfriend's hand as a man in public, I am not seen—we are not seen—as a queer couple any more. We're seen as a straight couple, and that was something that really bothered me.

JOE: Right. It's the irony of passing, you know?

IAN: Yeah, I don't want to say I'm invisible, because I'm not, but there is that vibe of, you can't see me anymore, and I re-ally liked seeing my queer brothers and sisters and being ac-knowledged by them and me acknowledging them visually. And now it's weird because I'll look at a lesbian couple or a queer butch/femme couple, and I'm excited to see them. I'm like, "I get you. I understand you." We have this shared experience, and I'm looking at them and smiling, and now I'm thinking, "Oh, they probably think that I'm one of those guys that's really into lesbian couples." They probably think that I'm that guy who has a lesbian sex fetish who takes a snap and thinks that's really hot. Now I'm the creepy guy, I'm not the trans brother. I'm not the butch sister or brother. I'm now the creepy guy who's looking too long. But back to the question of realness—it's not just straight people who are judging the realness of trans people. It is everybody in the LGBT community. It is trans people making those judgments on other trans people. I know that. I'm guilty of it. I'm not doing it in a way that I feel like I'm saying that somebody is enough or not enough. I definitely don't. It's through a different lens. I do believe that from my trans experience. But I do think it is all of our work to let go of realness and find acceptance, and you don't have to understand something in order to accept it.

JOE: It's about letting go of judgments, right? I mean there are a lot of judgments going on both in the cisgender world and the LGBTQ world, and I think that your point is acceptance doesn't require understanding because we're all human.

IAN: Absolutely.

JOE: Which is the fundamental point. So, Ian, I'm wondering. Do you see your humor continuing to evolve in different directions? Could you imagine yourself going in a direction where maybe gender identity becomes not as big a component, and you're going into a totally different unexplored area?

IAN: Yeah, I can see that happening—that maybe my humor becomes post-gender. It would be awesome. I would love to go out sometimes to an audience and not have to explain the 101 version of my gender before I do some of my jokes.

JOE: Yes, you could dispense with that whole piece of it and just launch into the show.

IAN: Yeah, that would really be nice to be able to do that. I can do that on college campuses where I've been hired by the campus LGBT group or a Pride festival in Houston or an LGBT comedy night in Columbus.

JOE: Where everybody knows you.

IAN: Right, to some extent. But what's interesting now is if I just mention that I'm transgender and don't go into the details, people assume that I am transitioning to female because there is this intense belief that I am male. So they think, "Oh, he must be transitioning in the other direction." Which is interesting too. When I talk to some audience members post-show, they're like, "Wait. I'm confused, so you're going to transition to a woman?" And I'm like, "No, I've been there done that."

JOE: That's amazing. Yeah, you've already done that I'm guessing.

IAN: Right. Yeah.

JOE: Well, listen, Ian, you've been really generous with your time. I appreciate this so much. You're just an amazing guy—so funny but profound as well. I mean that very seriously—in your insights into life. So thanks once again, and I just want to say Ian Harvie Superhero. Everybody go out and buy it.

IAN: Thank you, Dr. Joe.

JOE: Thank you, Ian.

> "If you are that attracted to me and you like my personality and you like the way I look, that won't change. Just because I have a vagina or just because I have a penis, who cares? We are one human race. Some women have penises. Some men have vaginas, like it's cool, and it's interesting, and this is what 2014 has brought us, this awareness, this knowledge, and we all have to co-exist. We are one race. So, what's the big deal?"

CARMEN CARRERA

Carmen Carrera is a reality TV star, fashion model and burlesque performer. In 2012 after she appeared on "RuPaul's Drag Race" and "RuPaul's Drag U," Carmen came out publicly as a transgender woman and began transitioning. She's an activist on behalf of transgender equality and is a strong and eloquent advocate for freedom and equality for all people.

———————

JOE: Carmen, I'm just so impressed any time I see you speaking. You're so articulate and passionate in your activism. And you really have an amazing story. You're always open and forthright, which is so hard to be, but you just seem to be that way naturally.

CARMEN: Yeah, I think it's because of growing up in Jersey and travelling to the city. You kind of have no choice, because everybody is so blunt, so you have to get used to it.

JOE: That's why I feel comfortable asking you about when you were a child. I know you've talked about it a few times. You said in one interview that you had the sense from a really early age that you were a girl—I think going back to kindergarten, Catholic school. And you told this one story that I thought was really heartwarming and charming—that you were attracted to a little boy, but not as a boy yourself—you wanted to be his girlfriend.

CARMEN: Yeah.

JOE: You know that is really very sweet. And I'm just wondering, you were such a young child—did you keep this sense to yourself? Did you communicate it to anybody? What was that like at an early age?

CARMEN: You know what—the way I was when I was young—I was very conscious of who I was. I was very in tune with my own spiritual reality. Being the Catholic girl that I was, you didn't speak about your crushes. You kept that to yourself. So I never really spoke about it. At the time, I didn't think that my body was a prison cell. It didn't compute right away. I was just being genuine. So if I had a crush on this boy and I would want to kiss him on the cheek, I just would. That was it. And I would smile and giggle, but I wouldn't dare tell anybody because I guess that's how the girls were in my house. My older sister, my mom, my grandmother—you just didn't talk about those things. It didn't really come together in my mind until first grade, when I was taken out of Catholic school and began going to public school. I remember a parent teacher meeting, and there was some kind of awkwardness. I just remember the feeling. I never could really hear what was going on. I was kind of oblivious because once again I was just being myself. I was cleaning up the whole classroom, I remember, and the teacher would always say that that's what I would always do is want to be helpful and clean up, and I just remember it being awkward energy. And that's when I really started to close up, because other kids would point out certain things about me that I guess weren't normal to them or how they were conditioned to see a boy.

JOE: I'm from the baby boom generation, and back in the day they had this terrible term, "sissy," which I hated. I remember walking home from school with this kid one day who spoke and behaved in what was viewed as a feminine manner, and we were talking politics. And instead of going home, he continued walking with me to my house. I lived just outside of Philadelphia, so it was a row home, and the houses were all packed together, and any conversation was very public, and my friend had a really loud feminine voice. We talked in front of my house for about a half hour. When he left and I went inside, my father immediately confronted me and said, "Isn't he a sissy?" Like, I shouldn't have been talking to him. I've always hated that remark. So there can be this really negative reaction from people . . .

CARMEN: Yes!

JOE: . . . if they look at a boy as being effeminate—to use that old school word—let alone identifying as a girl. So you're saying you sensed some negativity at school, and you decided to stay private.

CARMEN: Mm-hmm. Yes, I was very aware of it. When I wanted to express myself, I would think, "Wait, hold on, you know that you express yourself this way. You should not feel that nobody picks up that you're different." Because I wanted to just be accepted. Any kid wants to, so you just adapt. At the time, yeah, I wanted to wear girl's clothes, but I wasn't going to make this big stink about it, because I was like, this is how I look. This is how I am. I can't change it, so I'll just not show them who I really am and be who they think I am or how they think I should be, just to get through school. And it was miserable—especially as I started getting older, because I wasn't satisfied with the relationships that I had at school. Nothing was real. Nothing was genuine. Nothing was lasting. I didn't even go to my prom. I didn't get to have all those memories that kids have. I couldn't wait to get the hell out of there and find myself, and that's what I did once I graduated from high school.

JOE: It's really a dilemma, though, because straight people and cisgender people don't have to come out, right? I mean, if you're a boy and you're going into puberty and you're realizing you like girls, you don't say, "Hey, Mom. Hey, Dad. Guess what? I like girls." And certainly nobody who's cisgender says, "Mom and Dad, as you know I am biologically a girl, and I want you to know that I do identify as a girl." There's no coming out for straight or cisgender people. But that's exactly what people who are gay or lesbian or transgender have to do, and a lot of transgender people end up having to come out twice—first as gay or lesbian and then as transgender. It's very, very tough to do that—to have those conversations. So I'm wondering, Carmen, when would you say your family first perceived you as a gay boy?

CARMEN: Well, I don't know. I was very fortunate because my family just let me be. Even my boy cousins, everybody just let me be until I was old enough to speak about it. They never really tried to influence me to be masculine. I was doing it myself. I was forcing myself to be masculine. But when I told my mom, she was like, "Wait, what?" Like she was so thrown off, and I'm like, "Mom!" Because I would bring my really flamboyant gay friends to the house, and my mom never questioned it. My mom, she's very "OK, honey that's your friend. Have fun. Be safe." But she never sat there and said, "Are you gay?" or "Is that your boyfriend?" She allowed me to be who I was. So I'm thankful for that. But once I became popular on social media and my cousins and my family members would add me on Facebook, they would see the photos of me as a drag queen. I was doing shows with my friends, traveling around the tri-state area, going to different clubs. It was exciting. At this point my family members would see what I was doing and say, "Oh, OK, I guess he's a gay guy who does drag shows." And that was my process of coming out—just being out and living—not sitting down and having some awkward conversations.

JOE: But what I find interesting is that it doesn't seem that you experienced bullying or a lot of negativity, and you at least had the freedom to be you once you were doing the drag shows. And you were admired for doing your shows, and it was a glamorous experience and a positive experience for you.

CARMEN: Well, I experienced bullying from the other side, meaning I would see people in my school bully other kids. And I didn't say anything because I didn't want to be bullied myself. So I stayed quiet, and that guilt stood with me. Once I was confident in myself to be who I was, I was like, "Well, damn I should have said something. Those people are wrong." Now when I speak to someone who's going through some of the things that I've been through, I say, "You have to be yourself. You have to be strong, because once you are in tune with who you are and you stop letting everyone else affect you, no one can stop you because you're living your own truth." I wish I had this knowledge back when I was young.

JOE: I think we all feel like that.

CARMEN: Yeah.

JOE: If we knew then what we know now and we could go back, it would be a really amazing experience. But you are standing up every single day now. I always like to say that one of the most radical things anybody can do is to just be themselves, and you are doing that.

CARMEN: Right.

JOE: If you are true to yourself, you are standing up for freedom and equality for all people, but it can be hard when there's so little understanding. I'm just shocked that even people who are really well educated and progressive still don't understand anything about what it means to be transgender. For example, there was a lot of controversy about your interview, along with Laverne Cox, with Katie Couric, and I have to say I was really shocked at Katie, because she was equating gender with genitals, with having sex reassignment surgery, implying that's what makes a transgender woman.

CARMEN: With Katie, we had a long interview. I sat there, and I spoke about my man. I spoke about my stepdaughter. I spoke about my career. I spoke about my fears that I had to overcome. We sat down for a good thirty minutes. But the editors chose to only include certain questions. So I was a little disappointed because I thought to myself, I gave you guys so much, and that's what you decided to show. I know my fans on Twitter and Instagram were saying, why are we still feeding the ignorance. Why are we still catering to the ignorant people's perception of trans people? Why don't we cater to the people who are open-minded and want to learn something? Let's focus on those people. So, yeah, I think the media get too caught up focusing on the wrong things. They cater to the wrong audience.

JOE: Exactly. You shared an awful lot of information about your family and your relationships, and then the interview was edited down, and none of that was there, and there was just this conversation with Katie asking you about whether or not you had had an operation. The point of this project, the point of this conversation, is really to counteract all of that. What we're saying is look, we're all human beings. And we're doing that not by debating but by telling stories about ourselves. You tell a story, Carmen, about yourself that's human and that's compelling—like I was a child, I was attracted to a boy, but I was attracted to him as a girl—and that story could touch somebody somewhere who has that feeling. Or even if they don't have that feeling, they might stop and think, oh, this was a little child who was attracted to another child, and maybe some understanding and empathy will exist where previously there was none. I mean it's clear that some of these issues are really difficult for people to grasp. It's difficult, for example, for people to get beyond the whole binary view of sexual orientation. I mentioned to you the last time we talked that I'm attracted primarily to transgender women. There isn't even a word for that sexual orientation, right? People talk about whether you're straight or you're gay, and it's almost as if there's no word for being attracted to transgender women because people aren't even acknowledging that transgender women exist. And a lot of guys are cowards and don't want anybody to know that they're attracted to transgender women.

CARMEN: Well, the thing is that any man that's attracted to a woman is going to be attracted to a trans woman. Period. I don't know if that's my Aries freaking confidence, or whatever, but I know that I am very confident in the female that I am.

JOE: Well, you know there's this other weird thing going on that straight guys don't want to acknowledge. I did a little stand-up comedy, and I had this routine about how just about all straight guys are in love with their penis. I would say to the straight guys in the audience, "you know you're in love with your dicks. So why do you love a dick when it's attached to you, but you don't love a dick when it's attached to somebody else?" I've heard from a number of transgender women, that, as you say, guys who love women are going to love transgender women, but nobody wants to acknowledge that. We're still a long distance from that being acknowledged publicly. It suggests another topic I really wanted to ask you about, because you're so beautiful, and it's passing. Most transgender women and men obviously want to pass. They want to be viewed as a woman or as a man. But as soon as you pass, you're perceived as you walk down the street as cisgender. If you're a beautiful transgender woman and a straight man who might not be comfortable with his sexuality is attracted to you, you're put in a very awkward and potentially dangerous position. So what do you say? If they find out, they could have a very negative reaction. How do you handle that? I mean, no cisgender woman who has just met a man's who's attracted to her has to say, just so you know, yes, I do have a vagina.

CARMEN: Well, if I'm in that situation where a guy doesn't know that I'm trans, and he's interested in me, I know how to handle it from the start. Let's say that you are this guy. And I have a feeling that you'll have a negative reaction from me being trans. I'm gonna basically tell you from the start, "You're attracted to me. You see my hands. You see my body features. You see my face. You see my eyes, my hair. I'm going to make sure, I'm going to point all these things out and say, "This is me." When you come from that real, genuine place, it doesn't matter. It doesn't matter if you're trans, it doesn't matter who you are, like that's just how I think. Maybe it's just me being crazy or whatever, but I think that's how everybody should be. It doesn't matter if you have a vagina or a penis. It's sexual pleasure, and if you're gay, and if you both are satisfied, then it's like, it doesn't matter. If you are that attracted to me and you like my personality and you like the way I look, that won't change. Just because I have a vagina or just because I have a penis, who cares? We are one human race. Some women have penises. Some men have vaginas, like it's cool, and it's interesting, and this is what 2014 has brought us, this awareness, this knowledge, and we all have to co-exist. We are one race. So, what's the big deal? That's my view.

JOE: Right, we are all a part of the human race.

CARMEN: Yeah, I don't think about it as a survival kind of thing, and oh, my God! I don't let any of that bother me. None of that exists in my world. I mean I know it exists out there. I'm not delusional. I guess, there's just this confidence I have as a woman.

JOE: It could be kind of scary, though, if somebody is not comfortable with their sexuality and they get angry.

CARMEN: I don't think they would, I mean, I'm pretty sure that can happen, but when you're genuine and sincere, I just don't think that people will react to you with anger. You say, "Listen, this is what it is. I'm trans, and I have a penis. Or I'm trans, and now I have a vagina. If you want to be with me sexually and want to move to that next step, then we'll do that." But that's a conversation that you have with somebody. I don't have casual sex. I don't sleep around. If someone's interested in me on that level and I'm thinking about taking them to that level, then I'm going to be conscious about what

I say and how I present myself. Someone can be uncomfortable with it. That's fine. It's happened to me. I dated for a year when I broke up with my husband, and I've been in that situation where it sucks, because I was falling for somebody and I could tell that they were falling for me too, and it's real love. And then they decide to force themselves to cut off the love situation. So to know that somebody has the potential to be your boyfriend, and because of ignorance they choose to not go down that path, it sucks.

JOE: But you're taking absolutely the most powerful approach— to be honest and let people decide for themselves. They just need to come to terms with the fact of their attraction. What about though a totally different aspect of non-acceptance— discrimination within the modeling industry? Tim Gunn of Project Runway, who happens to be gay, was asked about the recent groundbreaking Barney's campaign, "Brothers, Sisters, Sons, & Daughters," which featured 17 transgender models along with their family and friends, and he said, "The fact that fashion designers would put basically adolescent-shaped boys or men in women's clothes is head-scratching for me because, anatomically, women and men have different shapes . . . to be looking at women's fashion on a tall, skinny guy with no hips, there's no way you can project yourself into those clothes." He's calling transgender women "men." I mean like what is up with that? Have you confronted any sort of anti-transgender views in the modeling industry, and, if so, has any of it come specifically from gay guys in the industry?

CARMEN: I feel like smacking people that do that. Shut the hell up, because you don't know what you're talking about. OK, this guy, I don't know if he meant to be hateful. Maybe he just views trans women as men because he doesn't have an understanding of who we really are. My first experience in the fashion industry was Fashion Week last September. I think some people were trying to look for what's fake, what's plastic, like that's how I felt. And I was all done up in my showgirl kind of like seal, just watching. But I think the fashion industry is open to the idea of using trans models. I mean, when I do fittings for designers, they're in awe of me, of my energy, I guess. They want to work with me. They respect me as a female, and a number of them are gay, so maybe it's just this one guy. One person can't speak for the whole fashion industry.

JOE: Well, in addition to the fact that he referred to transgender women as "men," what didn't make sense was to be putting down transgender models because they're supposedly too thin or aren't shapely when transgender women come in all shapes and sizes just as cisgender models do, and when that whole thin look in modeling goes all the way back to the 1960s with Twiggy, who was a totally straight and flat woman. I mean, you, Carmen, are very voluptuous, naturally, so what he's saying doesn't make sense from any conceivable standpoint.

CARMEN: Honestly, I always question my figure. It bothers me sometimes. I kind of look at myself like Oh, my God! If this is supposed to be a male body, like, is my body going to change? Are my shoulders going to get broad all of a sudden? Are my hips going to get narrow? I freak out sometimes. And then I think to myself, this is not a male's body. This is a female's body. And if I look at a lot of other females, I think not every woman is curvy. And the same thing with trans people. They do come in different shapes and forms. I transitioned, so there might be some features that are a little bit more masculine than others. There are times when I look in the mirror and I see a little bit of who I was before, but that's because

I allowed that to happen. Basically, I'm still going to look like how I used to, just a more feminine version.

JOE: Which leads me to another question. You're continuing to perform in the theatre, doing burlesque, doing drag shows. You began doing shows when you presented in your life as a man. Now you're doing shows as a transgender woman. Do you see the audiences perceiving you differently now that you've come out as transgender, or is it the same?

CARMEN: I don't even know. That's a good question. Drag shows are no longer what people think. It's not about a man in a wig, like that's old school. Instead you have your comedy queen. You have your dancing queen. You have your goddess, which is usually a trans woman. It's no longer a drag show. It is LGBT entertainment, and trans women and trans men are a part of our LGBT entertainment. When I go out to do my shows, I'm having the best time of my life because I can have a drag element and a burlesque element and a strip tease element if I want to. I can play whatever character I want to be. There are times when I'll crawl around on the floor, and I will take off my clothes, and I will be just as sexy as I want to be, while expressing whatever song I'm expressing. Whatever I do, everyone's pretty much been showing me love, and it's always love. It's always been that way since I started performing. It's never changed. So I don't know how my audience necessarily perceives me. I'd have to ask them, but it feels like it's a good thing.

JOE: Yeah, it's all good. People are just embracing what you do, so that's great. Now I know you've been traveling and a lot of exciting things are happening. What is down the road now in the next couple of weeks and months that you'll be doing?

CARMEN: Well, I'm working on developing my acting abilities. I'm the type of person that I need to experience everything for myself. Even if I don't do well, I don't care. I'm going to look at it, and I'm going to fix it. That's how I've always been with everything that I've done. I just kind of jump into it.

JOE: That's great. You put yourself out there, you know?

CARMEN: Yeah. I want to get to a point where I can play a trans and I can play a biological female. Why not? I would love to do that eventually. So I'm working on that. Also, I'm going back on tour with "Live Nation," so I'm revamping my whole show. And I have another spread that I just shot in London, for *S MODA*, which is like a really gay fashion magazine in Spain. So I'm waiting for that to come out. Those are some of the things that I have to look forward to. (Note: Carmen appeared on the cover of *S MODA in June 2014.*)

JOE: Well, that's great. A lot is happening. Well, listen, it was really just amazing to have a chance to speak with you. Thanks so much, Carmen.

CARMEN: Thank you, love. You too, take care.

DR. JOHN D. ALLEN AND THE RAINBOW SUPPORT GROUP

"The real message is that everyone shares the human need to have love and to give love and to receive love."

John D. Allen, Ed.D. has devoted his career to supporting people with intellectual disabilities. He is Co-President of the New Haven Pride Center and Co-Facilitator of the Rainbow Support Group for LGBTQ people with intellectual disabilities. Joining John and me in the conversation are Rainbow Support Group members Ben Nessl, Liz DeVoe, Pablo Cardona, Jackie McIlwain and Bob Hedlund.

JOE: I'm really delighted to be here with you, John, and with several members of the Rainbow Support Group of New Haven, Connecticut. I was wondering if we could begin by your sharing what led you to start the Rainbow Support Group.

JOHN: The Rainbow Support Group is unique. We believe that we were the first group in the country to support people with intellectual disabilities who identify with the sexual minority community. We started this in 1998, and the group continues to be strong and provide wonderful support to the sexual minority community and to help people understand that sexual orientation and gender identity cross all kinds of boundaries, including intellectual boundaries. Back in 1998, I was working for a non-profit agency supporting people with intellectual disabilities, and I started getting calls from people all around the state, saying "We've got an individual who likes to cross dress," or "One of my clients is gay, and there's no support group or way for this person to meet others like him, and is there a group?" So I made an exhaustive search for many months to no avail, and finally I said, "Well, gee, maybe the reason I can't find anything is that nothing like this exists."

JOE: There was nothing out there to support the needs of this community.

JOHN: Right. It was really amazing. And so we held our first meeting, and we had six members who came from around the region and staff, including several therapists, were there as well. Over time the non-profit community has become more accepting of this. We invite staff and family members. We have all kinds of folks that just come in and sit. We even have people who attend because of their affiliation with the community center and have no connection with a person with an intellectual disability. They come, and they participate. In fact, one of our longest-standing non-disabled members has no real connection to anybody with a disability. In addition, we've been creating a lot of the literature about the intersection of intellectual disabilities and sexual orientation and gender identity. We talk about staff practices. We speak at international conferences. There's a book out on our group.

JOE: So you're educating the larger community as well.

JOHN: Yes, and even though we've been going for a long time, I am amazed at how people still come to me, professional staff come to me, and seem to be in the pre-Stonewall age dealing with sexuality. Forget about homosexuality and gender expression, just sexual issues for people with intellectual disability.

JOE: Can you talk a little bit more about that issue? Many people with intellectual disabilities spend time in group environments. It seems that personal relationships are discouraged within those environments if they are viewed as romantic or if there is some level of intimacy beyond friendship. And that is undoubtedly even truer in the case of people who express same sex attraction. Can you explain why that is and how that impacts people who are living in group environments?

JOHN: It's so difficult for folks with intellectual disabilities to form friendships. And then to take that a step further, to form romantic relationships. For the primary reason that the folks often require the assistance of staff members to facilitate things that other folks take for granted. For instance, if you live on the other side of town or you live in another town and there's no bus service, how are you going to get to that other person? When it's about trying to find other people that you could have a peer network with? When you live in a group home and there are five other housemates there, the issue of privacy comes into play. Typically there might be one or two staff on for a shift with several other housemates. If someone wants to go off on a date, how is that individual going to navigate getting there, going out, making sure that they're paying for the dinner, making sure that they come back?

JOE: So there are practical issues, logistical issues. But would you say that there's also a point of view that militates against any expression of a same sex attraction, more so than an opposite sex attraction?

JOHN: Well, that's a very good point, and I think what happens is that while our profession is very client focused and professional staff want to make sure that the individual's needs and desires are taken care of, at the same time, we are all human beings, and we all come to the workplace with our own biases and concepts of what's right and wrong. Frequently there are folks that feel that being gay and having sex outside of marriage is wrong. They have those biases, and they might not fully support the individual. It's very easy to say, well, that's really not something that the individual wanted or their friendship didn't really take off. It's easy to sort of steer someone in a direction that maybe is not fully supporting their dignity and their human rights.

JOE: in addition though to the moral bias that you're pointing out, do you think that there's also a bias simply against the community of intellectually disabled people—that it's not that important for them to have intimate relationships?

JOHN: Oh, absolutely, and there is also the fear factor that goes on. People are fearful of any kind of sexual expression, not only because of the possibility of children or the possibility of sexually transmitted diseases. Some people feel that there's something wrong with folks with intellectual disabilities expressing sexuality or that it could be considered distasteful in some way. But we know that to be human is to want and have a need for sexual expression.

JOE: And to connect.

JOHN: And to connect with others. You know, I really want to say that in my experience of doing this now for sixteen years, that oftentimes we have our members come here, and they have no problem expressing their sexual orientation or their gender identity, because they're coming together in a group and there's a way that they can find acceptance. But what oftentimes happens is that they are reluctant to identify as a person with an intellectual disability. Because to have an intellectual disability is so vilified. It's more vilified than to be gay or lesbian or transgender.

JOE: Well, thank you, John. That's a great introduction to the amazing work that you're doing. So why don't we have the members of the Rainbow Support Group who very happily are here with us today introduce themselves?

BEN: Hi, my name Ben, and this is my girlfriend, Liz. And we've been going steady for what?

LIZ: Eight years.

BEN: Eights years. And we enjoy ourselves. Sometimes we have our little ups and downs. But you know young couples—

LIZ: We make up.

BEN: We make up.

LIZ: And we live together in a one-bedroom apartment in Hamden.

JOHN: Did you want to mention anything about why you feel it's important to come to the Rainbow Support Group?

LIZ: It's important for me and Ben to express how we are and how we act towards each other when we're together.

BEN: What she's trying to say is we always fight. That's because we love each other. But like I said, we don't come to the Rainbow Support Group with our problems. We come here for health support. Like I said, we're living here. We take the bus back and forth. We go to the library or any place she wants to go we go. We enjoy ourselves.

PABLO: Hi, I'm Pablo Ernesto Cardona Cerrano. I'm bisexual. I knew I was bisexual when I was a little kid. I knew I was different out of the street community. And I'm proud to be bisexual. And I want somebody to love me, not for my money or other things, just for me. I don't believe in cheating. I'm a very friendly type. I want to make friends and just meet and talk to people.

JOHN: You are very friendly.

PABLO: Yeah, and I'm independent.

JOE: And you travel all over.

PABLO: Oh, yeah, all over the state.

JOHN: And you're also politically active.

PABLO: Yes. I'm a political volunteer. I support gay rights and bisexual, lesbian and transgender rights. I'm here to talk to and listen to people in the support group.

JACKIE: I work with Bob. He and I have been friends for over twenty years, and now I work with him, supporting him in the community.

BOB: My name is Bob. I'm openly gay. I've had a very interesting life, but the reason why I come to the Rainbow Group is to express myself in an appropriate way. Also, to learn what is appropriate, what is not appropriate. I had a twenty-four year relationship with a partner. He died in 2002. Yeah, it's kind of hard to speak about it. It's kind of hard. I don't know what to say.

JOE: Well you're feeling very emotional, right, because you had a very close relationship with your partner and he's gone.

BOB: Yes. Yeah, he went, and it's kind of hard for me. I still live independently in the community. I'm supported by the Department of Developmental Services. Also, I have a job. And I'll be retiring pretty soon.

JOE: Where do you work, by the way?

BOB: I work for a flower shop in Bristol.

JOHN: But also in your earlier life you had been in and out of some institutions, right?

BOB: Yes, I used to be institutionalized. I kind of had bad behavior, aggressive compulsive behavior. I would act out. One day I just took a look at myself, didn't like what I saw and I changed.

JOE: That's great, because it's so hard for anybody to change anything. To change the things that can be changed and not just say it but do it.

JOHN: Well, that's wonderful, and, Bob, you've been a longstanding member, and so have Ben and Liz. And I just wanted to ask the group. Why do you keep coming back almost every single month, year after year? What is it about the group that interests you or that you get from it?

BOB: It's because I can talk and relate to other people like Ben and Liz, everybody else that's in the group. And I bring up things that sometimes I might handle wrong. But they will tell me. They say, this is the way you should handle it. And also, I like to be a pain in the neck.

JOHN: Like when we went to the Gay Pride parade in Northampton, Massachusetts, and you were just having a great time.

BOB: Yes, I got lost. I was embarrassed. What happened is, I was handing candy out to the kids. But I made sure there were adults there. And I got too involved in it. And what happened is, the parade just went on.

JOE: The parade left you behind with the candy?

BOB: Yes. So I had a very nice time. I kind of enjoy things with the Rainbow Group. And I remember the first time we went on a trip, and we got off of the train station

JOHN: In New York City. When we went down there to speak.

BOB: We went there to speak, and all of a sudden I look up, and I see these two guys, and they mooned us.

JOE: Well, that'll happen in New York City.

JOHN: Here we are in a gay group, and we get mooned in New York City.

JOE: Well, that was a welcome to the Big Apple.

JOHN: It was a wonderful welcome.

JOE: It seems that everybody here is living independently now. Bob, as you just said, you didn't in the past. Has anyone else lived in group situations before, or has it always been independent?

LIZ: I lived with my family for 32 years.

JOHN: Now how did you and Ben meet?

LIZ: Through a mutual friend in East Haven. She didn't want him anymore.

BEN: What she's trying to say is she was too old for me. I needed a younger chick. I need a young woman that has more pep and more—

LIZ: Power . . .

BEN: —in that department. Like I said, we take care of each other, and we help each other out, and I enjoy it, and she enjoys it.

JOHN: Now let me ask you a question. When you first came, Ben, you would talk about how there was another persona that you had, but when Liz started coming to the group with you, there was a little bit of uncomfortableness, but now it seems like you guys are pretty cool with whatever you're doing.

LIZ: Yeah. When I first met Ben, in East Haven, I didn't know what to think. You know, sexuality-wise.

JOHN: Why? Maybe you can explain a little bit about that.

LIZ: Because I didn't know what he was up to, and he kind of told me about Barbara. I was kind of jealous in the beginning, and I'm like, wait a minute. This was when we first started dating. And this was like a shock to me.

JOHN: Maybe you could explain a little about who Barbara is.

LIZ: She is his alternate ego.

BEN: She's my alter ego. I let her come out when I want to feel better.

LIZ: Yeah. When I first met her, I was a little shocked, but once I got to know her, she's been like a second sister to me.

JOE: So at first it was a shock that sometimes Ben is Barbara, but now you accept that, and it's part of your relationship.

LIZ: Yep.

JOE: And Pablo, you mentioned that you're bisexual.

PABLO: Yeah. Bisexual.

JOE: What is your current living situation? Are you living by yourself?

PABLO: I live alone.

JOE: Previously, though, when you were living with your family, could you talk about to what degree you were supported or not in terms of your sexual orientation?

PABLO: My mom is not that accepting of who I am. It's like she's trying her best, but she's not accepting like I want her to be.

And some of the family is anti-gay. Some are in the middle, and one is supportive.

JOE: So it's a mixed bag.

PABLO: Yeah, it's a mix.

JOE: And your mother is doing better than she did before?

PABLO: She don't accept the sex part. To me, what I want for my family is to accept me for everything.

JOE: Right, for who you are.

PABLO: For who I am.

JOE: Completely.

PABLO: Yes. Yes. Completely. And there are people who I thought of as friends who left me because I would open up and I'm bisexual to all the people I know. Half of my friends put me aside. They didn't want to be friends because of what I am. Bisexual. And they just ignored me like they never knew me. And some friends accept me, some of them.

JOE: How do you feel about the people you're calling friends who no longer accept you now that they know—

PABLO: I just forgave them. I don't hate. I dislike what they did. I don't believe in hate.

JOE: Well, that's a great response. And, Bob, you mentioned that you had a long-term partner, and you're now living independently. Would you be interested in relating any of your experiences of when you were in a group situation, the degree to which you were or were not supported for being gay?

BOB: I knew I was gay when I was four years old. But in my day, you didn't bring that up. And I always was under the Department of Income Maintenance, you know, through the state, the Department of Children and Youth Service. I met my partner in Connecticut Valley Hospital, and we started seeing each other. And he had the keys to Shew Hall, so we used to go up to Shew Hall and lock the door and stuff.

JOE: So you had some privacy.

BOB: Yes. And there were things that I did not like about him. There were things that I dealt with through the years.

JOHN: Well, the two of you worked together. You supported one another.

BOB: Yeah, we supported each other. There was one part of him I did not like, but there was the other part that I did like, and he was a very gentle person. But he had emotional problems. So I worked with him, and we worked with each other. And for twenty-four years we went through thick and thin, and we were always together till the end.

JACKIE: His partner was a very intelligent man and did a lot in bringing Bob to where he is today, I have to say.

BOB: Oh, yes.

JOE: Well, that was an enduring relationship, and I think everyone who's had relationships knows there are certain things you like and certain things you don't like about the person you're with, but you work through them. It seems that that's what you did successfully.

BOB: Yes.

JOHN: One of the things, Bob, that is so impressive about you is that you are one of the oldest members of the group, and you still have a tremendous desire to be partnered and have a companion.

BOB: Yes.

JOHN: And just how you have been so forthright in your approach to trying to find another companion to the point where you met someone within the group, and actually Bob and his friend were featured in a front page *Hartford Courant* article, where they were pictured walking hand in hand. Bob and he were making plans to move in together and that hasn't worked out yet, but they are still friends.

BOB: We're still working on it. We're still working on Timmy living with me.

JOE: So that's still a possibility.

BOB: Yes.

JOHN: If I may sum up, I think the real message is that everyone shares the human need to have love and to give love and to receive love. And I think that's something that we tend to forget in the profession, the need for having intimacy. And I would like to see the profession do a better job of addressing those needs. I think that we've done a great job of providing residential support and vocational support to enable folks to work in the community. But we tend to be lacking when it comes to the personal issues that really impact a person's quality of life.

JOE: Their relationships.

JOHN: Yes—relationships, friendships. And out of friendships can grow the potential for an intimate relationship. And that is so critical. That's something that we haven't done a really good job of supporting in the profession, and I would like to see that change.

JOE: Well, thank you, John, and thank you everybody for sharing your personal stories today.

JOHN AND THE GROUP: Thank you.

HINA WONG-KALU

"It's my personal goal to simply be myself, but in being myself, to show other people that I can physically represent what makes me feel the most comfortable. But I don't have to be defined and limited to the constraints of the Western understanding of gender expression and sexuality."

Hina Wong-Kalu is the subject of a documentary by Joe Wilson and Dean Hamer entitled, *Kumu Hina,* which in Hawaiian means "Teacher Hina." Hina is also a mahu, that is, a transgendered person. In Hina's words, a "mahu" in Hawaiian culture and tradition is a person who "straddles somewhere in the middle of the male and female binary." The film focuses on Hina's identity as a mahu, her professional life as a school teacher and an educator of Hawaiian culture and tradition and her relationship with her husband, Hema. In addition to being a teacher, Hina is also an advocate for LGBTQ rights. She was extremely active as an advocate on behalf of the successful effort to bring marriage equality to Hawaii and is an articulate advocate for freedom and equality for all people. She has twice graduated from the University of Hawaii and has been active for many years in a host of community organizations, including the Oahu Island Burial Council, having been a very effective community advocate on ancestral burial issues for several years.

JOE: Welcome, Hina. It's great to have the opportunity to speak with you today.

HINA: Yes, aloha. Thank you for having me join you in this dialogue. I'm honored to participate and to hopefully contribute by putting words and putting sentiment out there that will help others.

JOE: I really appreciate that. You know, looking at the clips of the film and seeing you in a number of interviews, I'm really struck by the fact that you seem to be a natural teacher and a natural leader. Did you always aspire to be a teacher and did you always feel within yourself that you had the ability to lead other people?

HINA: No, I did not aspire to be a teacher. However, I recall in one of my earliest memories that my maternal grandmother would sit with me with her hand over mine and at a very young age try to guide my hand and teach me to write. She said that I needed to pay close attention in school, because one day I was going to be a teacher. But I never had any real target to become a teacher, albeit from the time I was in high school I was actually groomed to be a student leader. But you really don't think about that. You don't think about elevating yourself to the status of teacher. For me, I just knew that I was assigned tasks and responsibilities that I had to fulfill. I come from a family that places a great emphasis on being diligent, being committed and following through on what is asked of you.

JOE: So hard work and dedication were values that you developed growing up through your family relationships, and that has led you down the path that you are now on.

HINA: Yes.

JOE: I was wondering too. When did you have the first opportunity to teach and were you excited about that?

HINA: I was almost on an actual progression of sorts. As I mentioned, I had been groomed from the time I was in high school to be a student leader or actually even before that. In elementary school, I'm not sure why, but I enjoyed participating in the student council. When I say I'm not sure why, it's because I was a very shy person. I think I joined in because I wanted to try to fit in with other kids. As I moved up to high school, I was still trying to fit in, so I was doing things that I was hoping were just going to keep me in a good place with a reasonable circle of friends. Once I graduated from high school, I went on to the University of Hawaii, where I became a teaching assistant and that sort of naturally led to my becoming a community Hawaiian language instructor after my graduation from the university the first time around. My first real engagement with teaching fulltime at a public charter school did not come until later. The director of the school came looking for me two or three times until I finally gave in and I said, OK, I'll do it. But up until that time, I had only been working with adults part-time and was not responsible for a fulltime teaching schedule. And so I kind of resisted. I didn't necessarily think that I was going to be effective working with younger students. But the last 13 years have proved that I am able to engage with them.

JOE: Well, you seem to command great respect and to have that kind of natural energy that attracts younger people to pay attention to what you're saying and to follow your lead. You mentioned that you were doing different things throughout your education to kind of fit in. And I know in an interview you mentioned that you were at times teased or bullied. Can you talk a little bit about what it was like growing up as you became aware of your gender identity? How did you navigate those waters?

HINA: I knew from a very early age that I wanted to, that I aspired to be beautiful, like my mother. From my earliest memories of my mother, I saw my mother, and many others around me saw my mother as a very beautiful woman. And bless her heart. I'm lucky that I still have her. But when Mom would leave me home to go to work, I often took care of myself. I was a latchkey child. I let myself in. I let myself out. I cooked whatever I wanted to eat. Probably from the age of seven or eight is when I was pretty much left to be responsible for myself with clear instructions on how to, what to, where to. As I said, I knew even back then that I aspired to be beautiful like my mother, and when she would leave, I would rummage through her closet and rummage through her shoe area—she had many shoes. And I would envision myself being in that way. I didn't necessarily think it was strange, and, as I got older, I didn't see it as me wanting to quote unquote "dress up" in the way that maybe people in a Western context want to do it. I simply felt that that was the more natural me, if I was able to achieve that. But I couldn't really say anything, because I knew that it wasn't going to be taken to very readily.

JOE: So you were just expressing your identity, but you did have a sense that you might not be accepted if you were expressing a feminine side.

HINA: Yes. And I wrestled with that in school.

JOE: Was high school challenging because of that?

HINA: In childhood I was teased for being effeminate. People also teased me for speaking proper English. Being a local child in school here, speaking good English meant that I was trying to be something that I wasn't. In the eyes of some of the others, it meant that I was trying to kiss up to the teacher, and it meant that I was trying to be separate and I didn't want to be with the local kids. But from an early age, that same grandmother who helped me learn how to write, she expected me—well actually my grandparents from both sides of the family—expected me to use proper English whenever and wherever possible. So it often left me isolated because I wasn't too skilled at the local dialects, what we call pidgin English or Creole English. Although I'm good at it now, growing up as a child I had a hard time with it. And I didn't fit in with the other kids because of that, and that wasn't even addressing the gender issue, gender expression.

JOE: But that's really a challenge for so many people—that whatever makes you different could become the reason to be teased or denigrated or bullied. It could be absolutely anything. That's why it's so important to teach the value of diversity and to celebrate our differences.

HINA: I am Hawaiian and Chinese predominantly, and there's a bit of Portuguese and English in there, and I am mostly identified as either Hawaiian or Chinese. On the Chinese side of the family, I was always considered the Hawaiian. On the Hawaiian side of the family, I was always looked at as Chinese. From the Hawaiian perspective, growing up as a boy in the family, I was smaller build. I wasn't as dark as some of the others, and I had less Hawaiian facial and body features. On the Chinese side, I was thinner than everybody, darker than everybody and I didn't look like an Asian. So I was always somewhere in between. As I said, I couldn't speak pidgin English very well, which meant that I couldn't really communicate and identify with people when I most needed to. Also, I might not have been good at things that those on the Asian side of my family were more attuned to, and I liked different things. So, on top of the growing gap of gender expression and discovering how to be myself, that made for an interesting childhood.

JOE: It seems that you were caught in between from an ethnic standpoint and then also as you were becoming aware of your gender identity.

HINA: Yes.

JOE: Could you talk a little bit about what it means to be a mahu? In the case of most transgender people, if you were born male, you identify as a woman. On the other hand, if were born female, you identify as a man. But you describe yourself as embodying both a male and a female spirit, male and female energies. Could you talk a little bit about that?

HINA: Well, yes. Remember this word comes from a time and a culture when there wasn't such a thing as SRS. You didn't have reassignment surgery. So having intimate relations with someone of the same sex, that's one element of the word "mahu," but another element is the male who assimilates his manner or dress to that of a female. Of course, we know that the word derives from a male dominated and male-driven sense of history and language. So there wasn't anything to address the female counterpart. But with that said, the word "mahu" applies to both the male and the female. And, living my life now, knowing the kinds of character traits, knowing the mental and emotional strength that I need by Western standards, I would be considered to be floating back and forth or in between the male and the female, so being mahu is to be someone who understands the perspectives of both, someone who embraces the perspectives of both. It's my personal goal to simply be myself, but in being myself, to show other people that I can physically represent what makes me feel the most comfortable. But I don't have to be defined and limited to the constraints of the Western understanding of gender expression and sexuality.

JOE: Precisely, and there are increasing numbers of people all around the world who identify as being gender fluid or gender nonconforming or gender queer or who do not want to subscribe in one way or another to the gender binary. They are simply presenting as themselves. And I think one of the issues that people have a hard time understanding is that not everyone is simply a biological male or female and that gender identity is different from one's biological sex.

HINA: Right.

JOE: And that people really live along a gender spectrum, and we are who we say we are, right? Gender identity is self-validating. If you say who you are, you have a right to be respected for that and to be believed. I know that you have said that you took refuge in being Hawaiian, and I thought it was specifically with reference to your being accepted for your gender identity, and I was struck by that, because transgender people are really marginalized in just about every circumstance. It's sometimes even dangerous to be transgender just walking down the street. But is there something in traditional Hawaiian culture that has created a context for you to be comfortable and to be accepted that one would not find in other societies and cultures around the world?

HINA: Well, yes. The social values that comprise the philosophical views of my people describe what it means to be HAWAIIAN. HAWAIIAN, to be someone who understands. HAWAIIAN, to love, honor and respect one another and all peoples. HAWAIIAN, to give one's assistance to others. HAWAIIAN, to take care of one's responsibility. HAWAIIAN, to be hardworking. None of these values are contingent upon someone's sex, nor are they contingent upon someone's gender identity and expression. On both the Hawaiian and the Chinese sides, to grow up in my family, to earn your place and to earn respect and acceptance, you had to be humble to your elders. You had to serve your elders. You had to know your place and know your time. There is a place and a time for you to offer what you think. And there is a place not. And it's not something that you question. There is commitment and diligence and dedication, devotion to family. And if you follow through with this, by virtue of that same cultural respect and appreciation, it would be challenging for my father or my mother to turn their backs on me, even though I may not be marching to the specific tune that they had set out for me. And that's exactly what happened. I transitioned from my father's son to my father's daughter over the years right before his own eyes. I lived in a house where I took care of his mother, my grandmother. I had to fulfill the roles and responsibilities, not from the perspective of being a boy or a girl, although based on a Western binary, the jobs I had would be associated with a girl. It was simply the job, and the job had to be done. The job was taking care of my grandmother and taking care of the house, taking care of responsibilities that are associated with running a house. So at age 15, I was given a car. I was allowed to drive. I was allowed to manage my time. I was told the things that I needed to do in order to provide support and care for my grandmother—whatever she needed. I was expected to do that. And if I did, I didn't have to worry about paying for a car, because it would be taken care of. I didn't have pay for insurance. I didn't have to pay for gas. I didn't have to pay for food. I could ask my father for whatever I wanted. There was great freedom in being pious to my culture.

JOE: So by being responsible and by embodying cultural values you gained respect.

HINA: Yes.

JOE: Regardless of your identity.

HINA: Yes.

JOE: Even among those who might otherwise have questioned it.

HINA: Yes, yes, yes.

JOE: So that is very important, that being responsible and true to your cultural values overrides ignorance and bigotry or just a lack of understanding.

HINA: And I'll take it further by saying that in my family, my father's mother was the matriarch of the family. She was the eldest of all her siblings, and in a large Chinese family, the matriarch of the family has lots of weight. So as I transitioned, the rest of the family watched me do this. When there were family functions and invitations were sent, most times adults only were invited, but I was always expected to receive an invitation, because if they wanted the matriarch of the family there, they had better have me there. Because I was going to be the one to get her ready, and I was responsible for her care. So, like I said, I transitioned before my family's eyes, and nobody dared say anything about the changes that they saw. They would comment, "Oh you look nice!" But nobody dared say, "What's that?"

JOE: So you got positive feedback, and you got support. And it's clear that that experience really prepared you to be a teacher and to mentor younger people, and I'm thinking about one of the key stories in the film. One of your students, who is a biological girl, identifies as both a girl and a boy and wants to lead the all-boy's hula team. Certainly you are the perfect person to work with that student and to teach the ability to lead, despite what other people might think. Could you just talk a little bit about that?

HINA: Yes, but I also want to be very clear that the film never intended to put my student out there as this champion for being gender fluid. I know that my student will navigate her way through the world no matter what's ahead of her. I hope that the teaching that she has had thus far at our school will tell her that as it was for me on both sides of my family—creating a place of acceptance but articulating that there are some expectations for you to fulfill. So you know that if you want to be a leader of a boys group versus leading a girls group, that it is OK. And it's not necessarily uncommon in our culture. However, there shouldn't be exclusion because someone is gay, lesbian, or anything else. And I say that because it's a very touchy subject for not only my students' families but local families in general. When they see their children growing up and straddling somewhere in the middle, the fear is that they won't be accepted by the outside society, not the local people, the local communities that we know and love, but foreigners. American people and Western people, Non-Hawaiian, non-natives. Knowing that Hawaii is dominated by non-natives, it can be extremely unsettling and disturbing to families to know that their child is going to be subjected to all kinds of things when we, in fact, love. We embrace. And we have other ways to orient ourselves, for example, just the idea of coming out or being out. In our culture right now it's hard for this generation to not embrace the concept of coming out and being out because we're so influenced by it, but when I quote unquote came out to my friends, the boys that I played sports with, they looked at me, and they said, "Mm, what's the big deal? Why did you call us in here for this big, dramatized meeting? You're telling us something that we knew from a long time ago. We were just waiting for you to get real with yourself. We thought that you were assembling us for something else." It was at the university dormitories that we all stayed, we congregated at, and they thought that

I was going to tell them some life-changing thing, that I was sick or something, and they were like, "That's all? You wasted our time to tell us that rubbish? We knew that a long time ago. We were just waiting for you. What do you mean come out? You just be yourself." And then they followed up asking me, "Do you have a boyfriend? Are you seeing somebody, and is he going to be good to you, and if he's not going to be good to you, then we will take care of the issue." That's the reaction I got from the boys that I played sports with in school.

JOE: Well, you never know what kind of reaction you're going to get when you share something that's very personal, so it's understandable to be concerned, but it's wonderful that your friends did support you.

HINA: Yes.

JOE: I think the lesson with regard to your student really is that everyone can achieve, even when others think that maybe they will not.

HINA: Yes.

JOE: And you can find strength inside yourself, because we can all be written off for a million different reasons, right? And in that regard, you have really been an empowering force for your student.

HINA: I always want for her to know that her skill, her talent, her personality and her ability should never, ever hinge on: number one, what other people think of her; and number two, the limitations that other people will impose on her. However she chooses to express herself, whatever fluidity she will have in her life, it's not for me to determine, and it's not for me to push one way or the other. It's for me to simply find a way to unlock her potential and harness it into something where she will learn to step behind her own reigns and get her own self running.

JOE: Exactly. I wanted to ask you in conclusion, Hina, since you've been so active in the community, do you have any projects coming up? For example, are you thinking of getting involved in politics or in other community activities in the future that you haven't previously been involved in?

HINA: Yes, I am campaigning for a seat at the Trustee table at the Office for Hawaiian Affairs. The position I seek is Trustee At Large. This is a statewide position, so I campaign on all the islands, and I need to avail myself of any and all activities that will get me ahead. I truly hope that by securing a high profile, publicly elected position, I will achieve recognition for myself as a Hawaiian, as a native person and also as a mahu. For all purposes and intents, people will acknowledge me as "she." They'll say "her." They'll use female pronouns. They'll address me as Auntie. They'll address me as Sister. They will address me as Kumu Hina, by the name that I have earned for myself. I will also be establishing that there is a place for people in the middle. And by gaining a highly public and political profile, I hope that I will represent to people on the margin of life, wherever they are, that they can succeed at whatever they put themselves to.

JOE: Well, I wish you great success in that endeavor. The work that you do is an inspiration. It's important in so many ways. I think through your life you express the need for acceptance and celebration of differences. And you're really every day making a powerful statement in support of freedom and equality for everyone. So I thank you very much for spending this time with me, Hina. It's been a pleasure speaking with you.

HINA: Thank you so much for having me. I appreciate it. Mahalo.

ASH BECKHAM

"I think it's really hard to not empathize with someone that you have a human connection with . . . it kind of evaporates the concept of the "other" and makes the issue—in this case LGBTQ rights—personal. I think that's when you really change minds."

Ash Beckham is a strong and eloquent advocate for freedom and equality for all people. She is a tremendous presenter who speaks about empathy, respect and the power of having real conversations. The videos of her Boulder Ignite speech on the phrase "You're So Gay" and her TEDx talk on "Coming Out of Your Closet" went viral, and there have now been over four million YouTube views of "Coming Out of Your Closet" alone.

———————

JOE: What I really love about you, Ash, is that you seem always to be focusing on trying to find common ground so that we can all come together and accept one another regardless of sexual orientation or gender identity, and that's the whole purpose of *The Human Agenda* project. We tell stories about ourselves. People listen. They empathize. They say, "Hey, that's sort of the way I am too." And I think maybe that is a way of trying to bridge the gap and move from tolerance to acceptance. So having said that, welcome. It's great to talk to you today.

ASH: Oh, thank you so much. I'm excited to have the chance to speak with you.

JOE: I saw an interview that you did with Niki Flemmer of "The We Belong Project," and she was asking you about your advocacy, and I thought you gave a perfect answer because you basically said you haven't been a public personality until recently but that you have lived a very out life for a long time and that you have always spoken out in your own life against injustices. That approach sums up what I've always thought: that the greatest advocacy is in living our own lives authentically, being real and standing up for freedom and equality in everything we do.

ASH: Yes, that's where we make change happen. I think it's really hard to not empathize with someone that you have a human connection with, so whether it's your friend or your co-worker or somebody else that you have that attachment with, it kind of evaporates the concept of the "other" and makes the issue—in this case LGBTQ rights—personal. I think that's when you really change minds. Because if it doesn't feel like it's your issue, then it's really easy to either be against someone who's different from you or to just abstain from having a position, because you just feel that it's not yours, but when you have this connection to a friend or a sibling or your kid's teacher or their soccer coach, for example, that's where minds change. We don't change them by advocating our position or giving the political justification for changing. We just be ourselves, and then it's really hard to villainize us.

JOE: It's that personal connection that makes the difference. We all know it's hard to change how anybody thinks about anything let alone something as fundamental but often misunderstood as gender identity or sexual orientation, but it's hard to hate when you know somebody and when you understand their story. That's why it's really important for us to continue to communicate every single day in a very personal way so that we can make change happen at every level. For that reason, it's great that you've always been advocating in your own life, but I'm also wondering what made you go public. It seemed to me from what you said to Niki that your decision to give the Ignite Boulder event talk was kind of spontaneous. It seemed that you sort of just did it. What was that like to just decide you were going to get up and give a talk?

ASH: Well, I had never really been into public speaking, but when I went to the Ignite Boulder event, I was absolutely enamored with the first speaker. It was a guy who was talking about his ups and downs with weight loss. He was so just real and awkward and quirky, and I just fell in love with this guy who was up there talking about his struggles. That's when I decided, OK. That's it. This is the creative outlet that I've been looking for. I didn't know what I was going to say. But I did know that if I was going to get up in front of a theater full of people—many of whom I knew because Boulder's not that big of a town—it would have to be something that I was passionate about. I've had this recent influx of children in my life—kids of family members and friends, kids that I'm really close to, and I realized that these kids at some point might have a tough time, because I'm gay. They love me, and at some point they might hear a slur, or someone might judge them for being with me, and it just killed me that they might experience that. You know, it's one thing to take that anger energy on yourself but to have it directed at a child because they love you, I couldn't handle it. So that was the genesis of focusing on the phrase, "You're so gay," to try to sensitize people to the fact that it's not OK to use certain words or phrases that are hurtful. Of course, I never expected my talk to reach so far beyond Boulder.

JOE: Right. And I think what was great is that you focused on a phrase that people use unintentionally in a pejorative way but which nevertheless reflects an underlying lack of acceptance in our culture of people who are gay. Ironically, the phrase is often used by people who think they accept people who are gay. That's why it struck such a chord.

ASH: Absolutely.

JOE: Because there are words that we use that unintentionally hurt people. Obviously there's also the virulently anti-gay Religious Right who engage in all kinds of denigration and demonization of the gay and transgender community and justify it through religion. But in either case, it's really very important to raise awareness about how language is used, for example, the distinction you make between tolerance and acceptance. We all think tolerance is great. But it's just one step in the right direction, and really it's a little bit condescending, when you think about it, to say, "I'm tolerating you."

ASH: Absolutely!

JOE: It's actually unintentionally demeaning to be tolerant. Even worse is the saying you "love the sinner and hate the sin." I consider that to be a form of hate speech.

ASH: Right!

JOE: When you say that to a person who is gay or lesbian or transgender, you're actually saying that the very way they are as a human being is somehow sinful, but you love them anyway. Or how about the use of the word "lifestyle?" If you're heterosexual, nobody thinks that's part of your lifestyle. If you're cisgender, that's not part of your lifestyle. If you were born a girl and identify as a girl, hello! you're just a girl, but if you're transgender, that's somehow a lifestyle. And in that context, the word "lifestyle" is used as a negative judgment, implying that you're choosing to be transgender. You're choosing to be gay and that that choice is sinful. Clearly, your sensitivity to language is part of what is making people respond so positively to you. So I'd love for you say a little more about the distinction in your own mind between tolerance and acceptance.

ASH: Well, I feel that tolerance is something we've always been taught. It's very baseline: just because somebody's different than you, don't hate them. There's no inclusivity in that. I feel that tolerance is something that is kind of mandated down, whether it's from a school administration or legislatively whereas acceptance says that a person who is different is part of the community. They're accepted and embraced into the community for the things they bring into our interpersonal interactions, whether that's a school or a city or a club or a team. "Acceptance" means that there is something innately positive and contributory about differences. For example, as I say in my speech, tolerance in your school district says sure you can bring your same sex date to the prom. We're not banning it, but then you go, and everybody stops dancing when you start dancing with your partner, so you don't feel comfortable going out there, and you're not allowed to hold hands. That's tolerance, but it's certainly not acceptance. You don't just want to be put up with as if you're something that can just kind of be put in a corner.

JOE: When you accept somebody, you're embracing them, and you're saying I honor and respect you for who you are. I think you've hit on a fundamental issue here about difference. I mean to many of us, being different is great. It's all about diversity. Why would we want everyone to be just like us?

ASH: Right.

JOE: But if you really drill down to the bottom of bigotry, what you find is that people discriminate against and are bigoted against people who are in a different group from theirs. They hate you if you're a member of that group. If you belong to a different racial group or ethnic group or if you have a different sexual orientation or gender identity, you're hated. Some people seem to see a kind of a threat in people who are different from them. That's why I think the whole movement toward trying to find common ground is so important. To me it's perhaps the best way of trying to move beyond equating people who are different with being alien or threatening. But moving to another issue, I was struck by the fact that even though you've had this overwhelmingly positive response to your TEDx talk, "Coming Out of Your Closet," there was one blogger, Melissa Onstad, who had a very negative response. Melissa's a lesbian mom of two kids, and her blog is called "Miles & Hugo & Moms." Did you see her blog response?

ASH: Yes.

JOE: She seemed to think you were equating the difficulty of anybody having an uncomfortable secret to share with the difficulty of coming out of your closet, which I didn't think was your intent. You were just saying, hey we're all human. We all have things that we're uncomfortable sharing, and that's where the common ground is, without suggesting that there's equal difficulty in all of this sharing.

ASH: Right, and I think it's really hard for any person to judge somebody else's difficulty. That is not even a conversation I want to be part of. I've had plenty of conversations with folks where my coming out story has been easier than theirs. It's fine to go that way, but to go the other way is really condescending and self-important. But what I was trying to get at with the speech was that there's no way as a heterosexual person you will ever know what it's like to be gay and to come out of the closet. You can imagine what it's like. You can suppose what it's like. You can come close, but you don't know what it's like. But I can tell you what it feels like inside of me, and if you can relate to a time in your life when you had that kind of feeling, then we can relate through that very common, almost animalistic connection of feeling that pit in our stomach. Then we have something in common, and that's a place to start a conversation.

JOE: Well, absolutely. And again, you can't judge the difficulty other people have in sharing something. Let's take something extreme. Suppose you are a heterosexual person, and you were raped when you were a kid, and you have a hard time showing love or trusting anyone else, and you have somebody that you really love, but it's not initially working out that well because you can't share that you were abused. Or that you weren't accepted by your parents for one reason or another or that there was alcoholism or substance abuse in the home, so I think you're totally right to try to find where the common ground is to get people who can't imagine what it's like to come out of the closet from a sexual orientation or gender identity standpoint to say, you know this is just a very human thing. Because obviously if you're heterosexual and you're a boy growing up, you don't have to say to your mom and dad, "You know Mom and Dad I like girls." That doesn't happen. Likewise, if you're cisgender, you don't have to say, "I was born a girl, and I identify as a girl." But imagine having to coming out about either of those things. You don't want to be rejected by your family. That's devastating, but you do need to tell them. Which raises the question, what was it like for you personally coming out?

ASH: It was challenging. It took me a while to figure out. In high school I was so scared that if I aligned in any way, shape or form with being gay, people would see right through me and know in an instant. So I was just scared. I grew up in Toledo, Ohio, in an upper middle class suburb, and we did everything we were supposed to do—like Mom and Dad stayed married and had two kids, and my little sister and I went through the same school system from kindergarten through graduation, and we played sports and all that stuff. When I grew up and went away to college, I told but didn't really tell my family because I was scared of what they would think or what they would say. I wasn't ready and spent the summer essentially lying to everyone I knew because I was dating this woman. And then she broke up with me, and I was devastated. This was the first time I'd ever had my heart broken in my entire life, and I reached out to my sister cos we were incredibly close, and I needed somebody to talk about it with. And she was amazing from the very beginning. She was incredibly accepting and was there immediately for me. Her biggest concern was taking care of the broken heart part. It's a blur in my head, but we didn't even talk about the fact that I was gay for days. At one point I was dating this new woman who was awesome. My mom is always so intuitive she knows when I have a crush on somebody even before I know, and we were having these very superficial conversations because I didn't feel like I could tell her, so we would talk about the weather or class or work or whatever, and then she pressed a little bit, and then I finally told her. It was hard for her. She knew a lot of gay people and was really comfortable with gay people, but her kid being gay was a different matter. She was just concerned for my safety, my wellbeing and what things were gonna be like. She was just incredibly protective. We decided not to tell my dad for a bit after that. When we told him, he really didn't care about the fact that I was gay, but he was born and raised Catholic, and so he had heard for years that homosexuality was wrong, so that was his issue. So my mom and dad had different concerns, but together they worked through it, and honestly they had to go through a coming out process with their friends, people that had been friends of ours and my family's for years, and it was not easy for them to tell their friends in the beginning. Eventually they kind of made a pact as many of us do when we come out—like OK, I'm telling everybody from now on. Like if anybody asks, I'm telling the truth, and this is, whatever, twenty years ago. So now my parents are incredibly supportive. Actually my mom is the one to go to in town for parents when their children come out, but it was a tough little stretch there while they kind of got their minds around this very significant change of expectation, a change in what they thought their daughter's life would be like.

JOE: And how long did that process take?

ASH: I think for them it was a couple of years. It was hard because I lived in Colorado and they were at home, in Ohio. At the time I was dating someone and we lived together, and my parents were great because they wanted to treat me exactly the way they treated my sister, who was dating a guy. We'd all go on a family vacation together, and my sister and her boyfriend had to sleep in separate rooms until they were married. My parents kind of held that same standard for me and my girlfriend. Also, my girlfriend, who I ended up dating for nine years, is an amazing woman, and the more my parents saw us to together, the more they recognized that. So all of their concerns kind of fell by the wayside. Like we were saying, it's those personal interactions—sitting down and having dinner together and having those conversations—that's what did it.

JOE: It's very important to come out. At the same time, it's a very personal thing in every single case, and it's very difficult. As you point out in your talk, everybody has to decide on the right timing—because there is great risk involved.

ASH: Oh, without a doubt. You don't ever have to come out publicly. Sometimes being able to look at yourself in the mirror is coming out. There's a huge safety issue especially for young people but also a lot of other people depending on where they are geographically or their financial situation. We need people alive and contributing. We don't need martyrs. You do what you can. I remember being so angry and frustrated with my friends back in Ohio for them for living in the closet and not being out when there's so much work to do, and I would think, why are you doing this. And then I finally realized (a) who am I to tell someone else how to live, and (b) these folks were doing everything they could given their various situations. So then it also meant for me that those of us that can speak out have a responsibility to do so for all the folks that can't. It doesn't matter to me why they can't. They just can't or they don't and that's fine. Everybody across the spectrum contributes to the cause. If all you can do is tell the person in the cubicle next to you that you have a girlfriend, then that is one more person that we're talking to about who we are. You know what I mean?

JOE: Yes. It's one person at a time, and we can't judge. At the same time every time someone does take that risk and exercises courage in their own lives and comes out of the closet and establishes new allies, it really helps everyone, but we can't judge people for when the timing is right.

ASH: Absolutely, I've always thought that safety is paramount— and not just physical safety, maintaining your job, for example. To me it is absolutely up to everyone's personal discretion.

JOE: As you travel around the country and speak, what is your core message now?

ASH: Now the message is giving voice to your truth. So I tell stories about my journey to where I am now. It's also that if you want to create an environment where everyone is almost beyond talking about tolerating and accepting and is moving on to celebrating, you need to figure out what your truth is and figure out how you celebrate yourself. When you figure out those secrets that you have or those vulnerabilities that you have, when you really look at that and you make decisions that maybe go against the crowd or you figure out the ways that you are different from other people and you're OK with it, that insight gives you a tremendous amount of empathy for other people going through similar self-examinations. It's a process for everyone, and so you have to give people a little bit of room to work through it. But the best thing you can do is figure out what your truth is, and by putting that out in the world, you embolden other people to do the same.

JOE: So celebration is the next step beyond acceptance.

ASH: Exactly.

JOE: Well, I think that is the perfect note to end on. Ash, it's been great talking to you. You're a real inspiration. You're doing tremendous work in your own life and out in the community. I really appreciate your time today.

ASH: Oh, absolutely. Thank you so much for speaking with me.

ANDRE ST. CLAIR

"You can refer to me as male or female. As long as you're not doing it disrespectfully, I'll respond."

Andre St. Clair is an actor, writer and activist. As a black, gay gender nonconformist, an immigrant of working class upbringing from Jamaica and a new American citizen, he is interested in nurturing non-mainstream voices and in promoting cultural and aesthetic diversity. Andre contributed to the anthology *For Colored Boys Who Have Considered Suicide When the Rainbow Is Still Not Enough,* which was edited by *New York Times* best-selling author and MSNBC commentator Keith Boykin. Andre is also a contributor to the *Huffington Post* and *theGrio.* He has a BA in Sexuality and Society from Brown University, an MA in Performance Studies from New York University, and a MFA in Acting from the California Institute of the Arts.

———

JOE: Andre, it's great speaking with you.

ANDRE: Thank you so much, I really appreciate it.

JOE: I was wondering if you could begin by talking a little bit about growing up in Jamaica and becoming aware of your sexual orientation and gender identity.

ANDRE: I was actually only there until I was seven. That's when my family moved to Brooklyn. I don't know when it dawned on me that it was not considered to be OK to have feelings as a boy for other boys. Kids experiment sexually all the time, but I thought it was wrong. I remember at the age of five I had my first sexual encounter with a boy two years older than me. We were playing house. I was Mommy, of course, and I used a t-shirt to give myself long hair and breasts. My siblings and cousins were our children. We did things that you do in a household, and as a married woman, I pleasured my husband sexually by doing fellatio.

JOE: And you were just five years old.

ANDRE: I was only five years old. So how does a child know how to do fellatio? It was something that I instinctually knew to do quote unquote in my role as woman and wife. So that was my first sexual experience, but I never told anybody, of course, and he never told anyone. Homophobia is pervasive in Jamaica, and it gets into the consciousness of the youth as well. But when I left Jamaica at the age of seven, I moved into a predominantly working class and poor neighborhood, East New York. It's like you leave Jamaica, but you're still kind of in Jamaica. What happened to me was because I was a new person and I was foreign and had an accent, I ended up feeling different for the first time. So I became a lot more isolated, because I felt misunderstood. Then a few years later when I was in fourth grade, I was getting a lot more feminine. I wasn't hanging out with the boys, and when everyone went to gym class, I always felt uncomfortable because I wasn't athletically inclined and the boys would tease me outside of the presence of the teacher, call me a faggot and a sissy. It wasn't until sixth grade when I had a husband and wife as my teachers that my academic promise was realized because they too were Jamaicans and they kind of mentored me. They were a Mr. and Mrs. Bailey, and I've never forgotten them. By that time, the taunting was just so prevalent. I remember one day one of my classmates was on this tirade, calling me a sissy and a faggot, and Mr. Bailey heard it and came up and said, "No, he's not gay. He's just a little different."

JOE: That was his approach to try to protect you, right? To have the other kids realize you were just a little bit different and not to focus on the idea of your sexual orientation.

ANDRE: Yeah.

JOE: Kids react negatively to difference if they feel more powerful than the person who's different from them. But implicit in your teacher's comment was that maybe there's something wrong with being gay, but you're not gay. You're just different, so there was that negative to it.

ANDRE: Yeah, but I don't think he had mean intentions.

JOE: No. But he didn't know how to handle it.

ANDRE: Exactly. Then a few years later an opportunity came for me to be placed in a program called "A Better Chance," which meant that I would be attending boarding school in Minnesota. My whole focus was on excelling academically, and it was easy there for me to hide.

JOE: You felt that you had to hide to protect yourself, that you could not let anyone know that you were gay.

ANDRE: Exactly.

JOE: Yes. But my understanding is that when you were younger, at one point you were wishing you were a girl so that your attraction to boys would be accepted?

ANDRE: Yes. It's not that I felt abnormal. I just wished I had been born a girl so I could do what I wanted to do, so I wouldn't feel the way I did.

JOE: If you were a girl and you liked boys, then people would support that attraction.

ANDRE: Exactly. Of course, a lot changed when I graduated high school and went to Brown and all of a sudden, lo and behold, I was around gay people.

JOE: So at this point you're identifying as a gay man, but from a gender standpoint you had not yet embraced the idea of being a gender nonconformist or gender queer.

ANDRE: No, I had not, but I was amazed to see all these people who were out and who had the support of the people behind them. So by the end of first semester I was fully out. But I was also getting depressed because every time I would go home, it was like I was de-gaying myself.

JOE: So life at Brown was incredibly liberating, but you would feel alienated at home, because you couldn't be yourself.

ANDRE: That for me was horrible.

JOE: When did you begin presenting as a woman?

ANDRE: There was an LGBT-sponsored party at school, and I decided that I was going to dress up as a girl. So I enlisted the help of one of my besties, Tehira. And she made me so beautiful. I remember looking into the mirror and just thinking, "Oh my God. I have never felt so beautiful in my entire life." From then on, I was dressing like a girl all the time, and because of my small frame and my feminine features, I "passed." I was getting validation from a lot of my friends and especially a lot of my girlfriends. They would say, "How is it that you are a boy, and you look better in a dress than I do?" It had not yet dawned on me that I was transgender. I was a boy who dressed like a girl. So anyway, for Spring

Break in my freshman year, I was supposed to go home. My spirits were so down. I felt as though I had to be gay. So I broke down crying, and I called my mom to let her know that I wasn't coming, and she got on the phone, and she was like, "What's wrong darling?" I'm like, "I'm not feeling well. I can't come home right now," and she was like, "Andre what is wrong? I'm your mother. Explain it to me. You always explain to me what's wrong." And I was like, "I can't tell you. I just can't come home right now." She kept pressuring me, and I asked her to guess what it was. She said, "You got a girl pregnant?"

JOE: Wrong guess.

ANDRE: I chuckled and said, "That is the least of your concerns." Her second guess was "You're gay." It took me a little while to respond, but finally I said, "Yes, Mommy, I'm gay." There was a little bit of a pause, and she said, "Andre, this is not what I would want for you. But you are my son, and I love you, and I will always love you. OK? Get yourself together and get on the next train and come here. You'll be OK." So I went home for Spring Break.

JOE: Were you able to be yourself on that visit?

ANDRE: Not at all. I couldn't be gay because my father was still not aware. Also, I attended an event at the church, and afterwards when we gathered at my aunt's house, my mother asked everyone to get together and pray for me. It must have been twenty people. I was literally put in the center of a circle. And I was just uncomfortable from the jump, thinking, "Why is this happening to me?" So I'm in the center of the circle, and I'm being prayed on, "Let him not be gay. Let him cut his hair, because they thought long hair was a sign of being gay.

JOE: It was almost like an exorcism, as if you were possessed and they were trying to rid you of the devil, you know?

ANDRE: Exactly. It was humiliating. Anyway, when I returned to school, I was cast in a play to portray a drag queen. And I loved it. I thought, "Oh my God, I'm a performer." This was also when I met Keith Boykin. He came to Brown to speak about his book, *One More River to Cross*. He signed my copy of his book and wrote in it, "Dear Andre, I hope this book serves as an oar to cross the rivers in your own life."

JOE: That's a great inscription.

ANDRE: Yes, and it became kind of like my Bible, and I brought the book with me on my next trip home. In any event, my father found the book, and when he did, my heart nearly jumped out of my body. When I was growing up, he would say things like, "Homosexuals should die, and if any of my children were homosexual, I would disown them." So he sees this book, and I'm like "Dad, it's for a class."

JOE: Which was kinda sorta true but not really.

ANDRE: Exactly. And he was like, "Throw the book in the garbage." Then all of a sudden my mom pops up, and I'm like, "Mom, can you please tell him that this book is for a class?" And my mom was able to diffuse the situation, which I thought was kind of incredible because my father doesn't listen to anyone. So he gave me the book back. At that point I wasn't ready to tell him that I was gay, but after I went back to school, I was involved in a meeting on LGBT issues where I was encouraged to be who I am. I felt supported and ready, so I called my father, and I said, "Daddy, remember that time when you found that book, and I told you that I'm not gay, and that it's for class. Well, that was a lie. I am gay."

JOE: Wow! That's amazing. You got to the point where you could do that.

ANDRE: Mm-hmm. And he went off. He was like, "Andre, if you are ever in Jamaica, I would have somebody kill you. You hear me, boy." That's what my father told me when I came out of the closet. And I was like, "Well, Daddy, you know what? It's all right because you've always been dead to me. It's been a long time since I've ever loved you," and I said, "I wish you were dead."

JOE: So the dynamic of that conversation was both of you wishing the other one was dead.

ANDRE: Yes, and the result was that he disowned me that day. And my mom didn't have any power over him to say that I could come home.

JOE: So you were totally cut off in every way.

ANDRE: Not from my mom but from him, but I couldn't go home. So I didn't see my brother either, and to this day I don't think about my father.

JOE: So you're still cut off from him after all of these years.

ANDRE: Yes.

JOE: Did that total break impel you or inspire you to just be who you are, and did you then begin to embrace the idea of being a gender nonconformist?

ANDRE: Yes, I did. Actually transsexual women that I was meeting were saying, "Andre, you pass. You should definitely take hormones," but it didn't resonate with me at the time. I was OK in my male body.

JOE: So you didn't take hormones, but you passed.

ANDRE: Yeah, my face is pretty. I'm passable.

JOE: Do you want to pass, or does that not matter to you?

ANDRE: It doesn't matter to me. But life is not linear. Recently I have actually been thinking about my status as a gender nonconformist. When I was in an academic setting, people would say, "Oh, yeah, gender nonconformist is amazing." But it's very hard to be an actor and be a gender nonconformist. So I am considering taking hormones and transitioning.

JOE: Well, I appreciate your sharing that. It reflects the ongoing evolution of who you are as a human being.

ANDRE: Mm-hmm, the evolution of who I am.

JOE: It also makes the point that as little as most people understand transgendered people, there's even less understanding of the concept of being a gender nonconformist. But with regard to the issue of passing, it's very interesting. As part of this project, I was speaking with Ian Harvie who's a trans man comedian. He made the point that when he began passing as a trans man, he felt that he had lost his queer look and that people were perceiving him as cisgender So it's a real irony if you totally pass as a transgender man or woman, people walking by you think you're cisgender, and that's what protects you. On the other hand, if you're a very beautiful transgender woman, and you have straight guys who are uncomfortable about their sexuality hitting on you, that becomes a dangerous situation, because they just hit on a woman with a penis. So it's tremendously complex from every conceivable standpoint, but if you're not trying to pass and you're dressing as a woman and people still perceive you as a biological male, that's very disruptive. People don't know what to make of that at all. But generally, Andre, it seems that on first impression, people view you as a woman.

ANDRE: Yes, especially if I put on breasts. They see my hair and my face, and I'm Ma'am, which is fine. I don't care either way. You can refer to me as male or female. As long as you're not doing it disrespectfully, I'll respond.

JOE: Of course, cisgender people don't have to discuss their genitals when they first meet somebody. Right? If someone is perceiving you as a woman and shows interest in you, you may feel you have to say, "Oh, by the way I have a penis."

ANDRE: Mm-hmm.

JOE: That's kind of crazy, but then if you don't say it, and the person gets more interested, you may be putting yourself in danger because you don't know how they're going to react when they find out. When they do, if they experience self-loathing and think, "Oh my God, does this mean I'm attracted to a man?" they could get violent.

ANDRE: It's happened to me several times, and it's always disconcerting for me because I don't know how to respond. Jamaican men can be extremely aggressive. The Caribbean men I know are extremely aggressive, and I've been followed, and I'm like, this is what women deal with on a daily basis. If I say I'm not interested, I'm still followed. It doesn't make any sense because I'm not trying to date the world. I'm walking down the street just to get from point A to point B, and I have a man who's following me to get my number. And some people think that when we're attacked, it's our fault because we're misleading people. We're not. We're people who are just living our lives. That being said, I have dated a couple of men who refused to see me as a man even after I took off my clothes. I still have the pretty face and the long hair and nails, and I have the anatomy of a male. I remember dating this one guy while still in college, and this was his first relationship outside of being with a woman born a woman, and he said, "Andre, I don't see you as a man. I see you as a woman, and I get pleasure out of pleasing you." So you realize sexuality is not just gay or straight. There has to be something in between because, here's this man who sees me as a woman but I have the anatomy of a man. So what is the mental process, the physiological process, that makes him attracted to me when he's attracted to women and not attracted to men?

JOE: I think you make the exact point—that sexual orientation and gender identity exist on a spectrum, but most of the world looks at it as binary. And that's just not true. It's simply a lie that almost everybody believes. There's the idea that you're either a boy or a girl, and that's the end of the story, but there are so many differences. For example, among people who identify as cisgender men, you have really macho men, hardcore men, and then there are very gentle men. There are all kinds of different cisgender men and women. But we don't look at it that way, and there still aren't words that really describe all of those differences.

ANDRE: Mm-hmm.

JOE: For example, I'm primarily attracted to transgender women, more than I am to cisgender women, and I'm not gay. I'm not really attracted to men. There's no word for that sexual orientation. And "gender nonconformist," I think, is a great term, or you could say "gender fluid" or "gender queer." But those terms are almost an acknowledgment that we don't have language yet to describe all of those differences. For example, there may be people who are quite different than you in how they identify from a gender standpoint but still call themselves gender nonconformist, right?

ANDRE: Exactly. I think the issue is understanding, even people within the transgender community understanding each other, because we don't have the language.

JOE: Yes, there are conflicts within the community, differences between gay men and transgender women and even differences within the group that we'll call trans and gender nonconformist. And maybe the differences are resulting in part from an absence of language, which reflects an absence of understanding.

ANDRE: And will we ever get that language?

JOE: Well, I think, Andre, by sharing so openly your personal story, you are helping to create that language and create a greater understanding of gender identity, of sexuality and ultimately of what it means to be human. So thank you so much for spending this time with me today. I really appreciate it

ANDRE: Thank you, Joe.

RABBI AMY BERNSTEIN

"We're binary about everything now. It's not shocking to me that we're binary about gender. We are locked into right/wrong, left/right, Republican/Democrat."

Rabbi Bernstein serves as Senior Rabbi at Kehillat Israel, also known as KI, in Pacific Palisades, California. She attended the Reconstructionist Rabbinical College in Philadelphia for her rabbinic training, which included one year as a visiting graduate student at Ben Gurion University of the Negev in Israel. Before coming to the Los Angeles area, Rabbi Bernstein served as the rabbi of Temple Israel in Duluth, Minnesota. She also served two terms as the president of the Arrowhead Interfaith Council and was on the board of trustees of the College of St. Scholastica. In addition to her pulpit work at KI, Rabbi Bernstein has a broad profile, including teaching and community service. She lives in the Palisades with her partner Judy, her daughter Eliana and their rescue Chihuahua Olivia.

JOE: Thanks so much, Rabbi Bernstein, for being generous with your time and spending a few minutes with me today.

RABBI BERNSTEIN: It's a pleasure.

JOE: I was wondering if you could begin by talking a little bit about your personal spiritual journey and what led you to become a rabbi in the Reconstructionist Church.

RABBI BERNSTEIN: I grew up in Atlanta, Georgia, and attended a private Jewish day school. My daily life was largely a Jewish life. The day-to-day life that I led was one with a Jewish vocabulary and a Jewish relationship to time and to what one does at what points in the day. So I think early on there wasn't a question about living an actively Jewish life in the Jewish community. I went to an orthodox yeshiva high school in Atlanta to continue my education. I loved the rituals of the day. I loved reading and speaking Hebrew and having a relationship to prayer and to a community based on ethics and values and history. But it was during my experience at yeshiva high school that I started to question, at least the orthodox end, of Jewish practice and Jewish theology. I began asking some hard questions about why don't girls wear a prayer shawl, why don't girls wear a kippah, why can't girls study Talmud—questions that made my rabbis very uncomfortable, and they seemed to have kind of the standard answer for those questions that I was less and less satisfied with. So, for me, leaving a Jewish world was the bigger question rather than why be drawn to it. The rupture came at about the age of 16. I could no longer stay within an orthodox framework, and I was really heartbroken—that I was not buying what my rabbis were telling me, that they believed some things that were to me outside of what was rational or even spiritually made any sense, that these were the same people who taught me other things that were so fundamentally true. As I said, it was heartbreaking to leave, so for me it was about finding my way back through a reconstructionist synagogue, after much searching and much failing at finding a really deep-grounded, immersed Judaism that spoke to my deep love of tradition and ritual and liturgy and that also spoke to my progressive American values.

JOE: It seems that what you sought and found is really something that many people who were raised within traditional institutional religions have had a very difficult time finding.

RABBI BERNSTEIN: It's really true—people who are like-minded in terms of issues regarding gays and lesbians and feminists, people who are pushing boundaries in all kinds of ways, particularly within religious institutions. I've really felt their pain. Those who were raised in, let's say, the Catholic Church or other branches of religion where you don't have a liberal expression that also feels like an expression of deep religious integrity. And I don't mean that philosophically or theologically. I mean the smells and bells. The real deep commitment to high church rituals. And I've really felt their pain, and I was there. I remember feeling exactly the same pain. And I do not take it for granted one single day that I walk into this synagogue. That I have, thank God, been raised in a tradition with a heart that loved it and that also has a progressive expression.

JOE: Certainly there's a commitment to the value of equality within the Reconstructionist view of Judaism, whereas you saw the contradiction within Orthodox Judaism. I was raised a Catholic, and there's a profound contradiction there as one gets older and realizes that the Catholic Church opposes homosexuality. And yet for reasons that are still not well understood, there are many gay priests. Also, of course, the attitude that many of the institutional religions have towards women, including orthodox Judaism, Islam and fundamentalist Christian denominations. These attitudes and beliefs have really been a great challenge for people in the LGBTQ community, not only because it's profoundly disturbing to be rejected and condemned by one's religion but also because a lot of times that rejection filters into the family too.

RABBI BERNSTEIN: Right.

JOE: That is, one's family continues to embrace that set of beliefs and then based on those beliefs, rejects the son or the daughter.

RABBI BERNSTEIN: Right. It's extraordinarily painful to have a heart that is responsive to a faith tradition, to have a heart that's so sensitive and open to connecting with the divine and then have one's closest family use that very precious treasure, that vulnerable, wonderful, amazing, awesome force, to condemn one out of what is supposed to be love. That is a crazy torture to the soul that is just existentially, horribly painful.

JOE: Well, it's my view that a lot of people justify their own bigotry by basing it on their religious beliefs. That's sort of a way out. To rationalize it.

Do you agree with that? For example, the rhetoric from a lot of the people on the Religious Right, religious fundamentalists, is extremely hostile and really tends at times towards hate speech.

RABBI BERNSTEIN: Yes. Right wing, fundamentalist Christianity or fundamentalist Islam or any kind of any kind of fundamentalism is uniquely suited to be used by bigots. Of course, the fascists and the communists haven't needed religion to justify their hatred. The Nazis didn't need religion, thank you very much, to exterminate millions of people. I think whatever excuse, whatever system, whatever authority, whatever way one can find to justify one's oppression of the other, it has been readily available in human societies of every kind. Religion is one of them, and it's a particularly good one, because who's going to say No?

JOE: But you have shown that courage. I try to do the same in my own life, because you do risk separating yourself from family, from friends, from community when you no longer embrace their beliefs. I think it's interesting that KI embraces the view that Judaism is an evolving religious civilization. It can be dangerous when people embrace a static set of philosophical or religious beliefs that they equate with the truth or believe that their literal interpretation of scripture reflects the thinking of the creator of the universe. And that's your guide to how to live in this world.

RABBI BERNSTEIN: Right. The minute one locates the actual words in a divine being, we have a problem if you ask me anyway. This is my interpretation, obviously, as a Reconstructionist. One of my teachers, Rabbi Jacob Staub, taught us—and I love this to this day—that there was something that happened at Sinai. The Jewish people had an encounter with the divine at Sinai. And what we have handed down to us is the record of our side of that conversation. So it's not the divine, right? It's not the word of God we have in Torah, in scripture. It's the word of the Jewish people in conversation with the divine.

JOE: So, to your point, there's only a partial record of what may or may not have transpired.

RABBI BERNSTEIN: So they heard voices. What does that even mean? We don't know anything about what that means. Because the encounter with divinity is ineffable by its very nature. What we do is translate that into words and ideas as human beings. And that's our job and what we have to do. But we are in very serious trouble, I believe, when one does not understand that conversation is ongoing and when one does not see it as evolving in terms of its implications. I also think that in the phrase "an evolving religious civilization," civilization is as important as religion—that is, our culture, our history, our language, our world view, our art, our music, our literature.

All of that goes to make up a civilization. There is a religious expression of a people as well, but it's not the entirety of what it means to be Jewish. And that is something that distinguishes the Jewish people and their religious expression from, let's say, Christianity, which is based on a set of religious beliefs. That becomes in itself a problematic thing for we who are LGBT folk. You don't believe something and therefore you're Jewish. Rather, the Jewish religious tradition grows out of the experience of the Jewish people.

JOE: Speaking of evolution and progress, there has clearly been a lot of progress with respect to public support for marriage equality. I was wondering how you interpret that. For example, in some of the conversations I've had about marriage equality as part of The Human Agenda project, we've discussed the difference between tolerance and acceptance and the distance between tolerance and equality. How do you interpret what is clearly a set of breakthroughs in various states with marriage equality? Do you equate that with true acceptance or not?

RABBI BERNSTEIN: That's a good question. I believe that in part it's been the courage of the people on whose shoulders we stand, who went before us, who lived their lives as out gay people when it was still so incredibly dangerous and risky to do so, that produced enough of us who could live out. I mean, I came out at 16. So enough of us felt safe enough to come out and live our lives openly. I really do believe we reached a tipping point where the courts would have to rule against too many Americans who want civil rights. And enough people have been raised in a generation of acceptance who, frankly, don't care very much about the LGBT issue. It's much more about the Q issue for this generation. It's much more that gender's not binary. We old gay people are just boring and totally a thing of the past. So that's a great development. I think if you combine the attitude of the younger generation with the number of people who are living out and proud lives, there's just no way that the court could continue to rule against that many people who say, A, we support it, and, B, I'm living it.

JOE: But it is certainly a long road. You mentioned people identifying as queer or transgender. I'm continually shocked by how little understanding there is of the concept of gender identity. There are so many well-educated, otherwise progressive people who just don't understand it at all or else equate being transgender with having had sexual reassignment surgery. They don't understand that gender identity is different from biological gender—that it's how human beings experience and present their gender. If you look at it that way, you can see that there are great differences even among people who present or identify as cisgender just as there's a spectrum of sexual orientation as well. But we're still locked into this binary way of breaking down sexual orientation and gender identity.

RABBI BERNSTEIN: Right. And it's symptomatic of our society. We're binary about everything now. It's not shocking to me that we're binary about gender.

We are locked into right/wrong, left/right, Republican/Democrat. We're so religious or so absolutely against religion. We are so locked into a binary structure of thought that it is really frightening to me. In the feudal world community, you look at radical Islam. You look at ISIS, and you think, we could not be more stuck in this—

JOE: Polarization.

RABBI BERNSTEIN: Yeah, it's really something. And people like Karen Armstrong believe that we are maybe looking at the emergence of another Axial Age. That we are right at the edge as human beings of taking another huge leap. And that some of this is a reaction to what people know is coming.

JOE: I was just going to ask you about that. And this is really, I think, a great challenge. Whenever there is progress, you always get backlash. I especially see that again in the rhetoric of the Religious Right and the demonization of gay people, lesbian people, transgender people. How do you deal with the backlash that inevitably comes with progress?

RABBI BERNSTEIN: I have not taken a particularly courageous approach to that. What I do is I just live my life inside my little bubble. I feel like living out and being the religious authority for a thousand family mainstream congregation on the west side of Los Angeles is my radical statement. And it's going to be up to my allies, my straight allies, other gay people who are living in different contexts to deal with the backlash. I really just feel like I need to be living my life as a lesbian, being in a position that's, A, male identified, B, God identified—a very traditional role, taking my congregation to the places I know that I can take them. That's my work. It's going to be somebody else's work to deal with the idiots.

JOE: But you are being true to yourself. You are being who you are. If we all had the courage to be authentic, to be ourselves, to stand up and just be who we are every single day, then the world would be transformed.

RABBI BERNSTEIN: Thank you. You make me feel like I'm a little less hiding.

JOE: You are courageous. You're standing up for who you are. You're authentic. You're living your life. You're leading other people. It is a male-defined role. You're speaking the truth as you see it whether others agree with you or not. For example, I'm an atheist. We don't agree on religious issues, but we agree on the values of freedom and equality and finding common ground. The reason I'm doing this project and I'm calling it The Human Agenda is that I think when people tell stories about themselves, it's a less divisive approach to some of these issues. I'm happy to write articles and to debate. And I've written a satire of The Bible called *You Got to Be Kidding*, which is very radical, and I've written a satirical memoir of growing up Catholic called *Papal Bull*. But those are simply perspectives. Another perspective is let's find common ground and tell stories about ourselves. That we're all really looking for the same things as human beings. That it's the human agenda as opposed to that horrible hate phrase, the homosexual agenda.

RABBI BERNSTEIN: Exactly. And that's where I think a lot of people are, which is why we're seeing what we're seeing in this country. I believe that a lot of people do get it, that it's the human agenda.

JOE: But there still seems to be resistance to lesbian and gay couples coming together, forming families and being parents, which is profoundly shocking. I wrote an article about a year ago for the *Huffington Post* about the fact that so many hate groups actually seize upon the word "family" and associate themselves with family values. There are dozens of them like Family Research Council and the American Family Association. What are your views on forming families as a lesbian? And why do you think there is so much resistance to that, as if gay and lesbian people are somehow a danger to children—which is preposterous?

RABBI BERNSTEIN: I honestly have zero clue what that is about. I can only imagine that it is about some underlying, very serious stuff about homophobia that people are not even aware of until it comes to the question of children. Because if you ask them, they cannot give you rational answers.

JOE: Well, there is no rational answer.

RABBI BERNSTEIN: Exactly. I'm reading a book called *The Righteous Mind*. It's about how otherwise intelligent, rational fully functional human beings can make these crazy leaps to justify their own reaction to something like gays shouldn't raise children. That they're in every other way normal, wonderful, amazing human beings who are very intelligent. And maybe even socially fairly liberal.

But when it comes to a question like that, they will go to any lengths to defend their answer. Because it's not a rational view. There's some kind of emotional content underneath all that that drives the reaction. What that is I honestly do not know. But what makes me want to weep, whenever the question comes up, is knowing that there are over 50,000 children in L.A. who do not have a home. And we have to even be in conversations about should gay people be allowed to adopt? Or to foster? Or to have their own children? I do not understand it.

JOE: Well, of course, people who take that position sometimes use phrases like "children do best with a mother and a father." Well, that's true except for the billions of times it's not true. What about the abusive households with a mother and a father? And of course single parents can be great, loving, heroic parents. I'm a single parent, not that I'm heroic. I'm just saying that children can thrive under many circumstances. Sometimes they grow up with their grandparents.

Sometimes they grow up with a gay couple. That's not the issue. The issue is love. Children do best when they're loved. And you're right. There is something really disturbing about what is prompting people to condemn people who are loving parents.

RABBI BERNSTEIN: Right. I don't understand it at all.

JOE: It is very difficult to understand. Well, you're dong wonderful work. I was wondering if we could conclude by your sharing some of your current projects and initiatives.

RABBI BERNSTEIN: One of the things for me that's really important is learning to talk across this binary conversation that we are stuck in on so many issues and so many levels. Taking a thousand family congregation, we are a pretty broad spectrum of political and other kinds of attitudes about things like Israel or the president. We include very successful people, which means they are often high powered. You know, very intellectual, very driven. And because they are at the top of their field, they are people who are strong and are ready to push their agenda. And when you get a bunch of those people in a room on opposite sides of these binary issues, you get these incredible reactions. It's getting worse and worse. I think more and more things are falling into that category of people hearing a word, and they have this emotional response that is not rational. So my job is seeing how we hold a conversation with people that we fundamentally disagree with on some pretty passionate issues and still treat one another with respect. That's a big one for me right now, because I think it's a big problem in the country and the world. I'm also involved in mindfulness practice. I do a meditation class every Friday after my regular Bible study. The goal is to find the ways we can just settle down and become less reactive and more responsive.

JOE: I think seeking unity in diversity and finding common ground is really one of the great goals to pursue these days, because we are much too polarized. But I really appreciate the work you're doing. And I thank you so much for spending a few minutes with me today to share your thoughts and experiences.

RABBI BERNSTEIN: Well, keep up the good work. And thank you for bringing these issues so wonderfully and thoughtfully to light.

JOE: Thank you so much, Rabbi Bernstein.

DR. CARYS MASSARELLA

"One of the really important messages about transgender identity is that being transgender is not biologically hazardous."

Dr. Carys Massarella is an attending emergency physician at St. Joseph's Health Care in Hamilton, Ontario. She's also the lead physician for the Transgendered Care Program at Quest Community Health Center in St. Catherine's, Ontario, and is an Assistant Clinical Professor at the DeGroote School of Medicine. Dr. Massarella lectures widely on transgender health and identity issues and has done two TEDx talks, "The Depathologization of Trans Identity" and "The False Narrative of Deception." She is the first transgendered person to be president of a large teaching hospital medical staff anywhere in the world and was named one of the world's 50 transgender icons by the *Huffington Post*. She's also a member of the gender advisory committee for gender in-dependent children for Rainbow Health Ontario, is a member of WPATH, the World Professional Association for Transgender Health and was recently appointed to the board of CPATH, the Canadian Professional Association for Transgender Health.

––––––––––

JOE: It's an honor to speak with you, Dr. Massarella. You're doing tremendous work, fundamental work, crucial work for the transgender community.

DR. MASSARELLA: Thank you very much.

JOE: I want to begin by getting right to the heart of one of the issues that you have advocated on so eloquently in a number of your public speaking engagements. You've made the point in a very compelling way that transgender people are not being well-served by the medical community and that this poor treatment is directly related to the fact the community pathologizes transgender people. Could you elaborate on that?

DR. MASSARELLA: Yes, absolutely. I think one of the really important messages about transgender identity is that being transgender is not biologically hazardous. What I mean by that is somebody who identifies as transgender suffers no ill biological effect. You don't get heart disease. Your cholesterol doesn't go up. Essentially what the medical community has done is taken on an identity and made it into an illness. As physicians, the way we're taught is that when we see something as an illness, our first thought is to cure. When we think of cure in this case, what we think of is that we can make somebody not transgendered or in a sense repair their transgender identity. In fact, we know from evidence that this is indeed harmful.

JOE: Well historically the medical community, specifically the psychiatric community, has identified transgender people as having gender identity disorder.

DR. MASSARELLA: Correct.

JOE: They now have in the latest diagnostic manual a kinder, gentler version of that called dysphoria.

DR. MASSARELLA: Correct.

JOE: Which to me is absurd, because if there weren't lots of people who were dysphoric about their bodies, plastic surgeons and medical spas would be going out of business. So lots of people are uncomfortable about their bodies and don't consider it to be a pathology.

DR. MASSARELLA: Exactly.

JOE: You make the fundamental point that when you pathologize somebody's identity, you say that there is something wrong with them at their core, just being the way they are, when in point of fact, identity should be self-validating. In other words, people should accept and respect who I say that I am. There's really no reason to doubt that, and yet that is what transgendered people face every day, which is why many transgendered people are afraid to go to a physician. A transgender person may think I have flu-like symptoms or I have chest pains, but I don't want to go to my doctor because my doctor is going to look at me as if I have a mental health issue, not that I just have the flu.

DR. MASSARELLA: Exactly, and in fact we published a paper this year in the Annals of Emergency Medicine, which shows that transgender people avoid even going to emergency departments with perceived emergencies because of the way that they're treated. So even with potentially life-threatening conditions, transgender people are avoiding seeking health care, because they know that when a transgender person presents to a doctor, all the doctor wants to talk about is their gender identity.

JOE: You also make the point that many physicians are very poorly trained. All they know is this reference in the Diagnostic Handbook. In fact, you mentioned in one of your talks that you were treating a client who was afraid to see another doctor because they thought they might be fired or not served by that physician, which is something I'd never heard of, the concept of being fired by a doctor. Why would a doctor not want to see a transgender person? Would it be that they don't feel qualified? What's the basis for that rejection?

DR. MASSARELLA: I think there could be a couple of reasons. One is their lack of understanding, although there are many conditions that physicians aren't comfortable treating, and which they'll refer to specialists, so they don't typically fire their patients because they don't feel comfortable treating a condition. I think a lot of it has to do with an essential bias against transgender people. In fact, recently I had a client who had gone to their family doctor, and the doctor told him that if he went to church or went to pray, that he probably could get rid of this identity and that it was fundamentally wrong. So it's still a perceived disorder by so many doctors, and doctors for the most part will refer transgender people to mental health providers who are not qualified to help them with transition.

JOE: In addition to the pathologizing of transgender people, as you point out in your other TEDx talk "The False Narrative of Deception," there's this bias that somehow transgender people are being deceptive, that if you present as a transgender woman you're somehow fooling people, because you were born with a penis. In fact, I was thinking about you yesterday when I saw a news story that a teenager in South Carolina went to get his driver's license—

DR. MASSARELLA: Yes, I read that.

JOE: Yes! That a teenager who was wearing makeup was told that he couldn't have his picture taken for his driver's license and that he therefore couldn't get his license because he was wearing a disguise—the disguise being the makeup and the lipstick. So there seems to be a kind of visceral discomfort that some people feel towards transgender people, and it seems to me to be based in part on that fact that people confuse biological sex with gender identity, that they don't even have a concept of gender identity and to your point that they equate one's gender with one's genitals, which is really demeaning.

DR. MASSARELLA: I think your point is exactly correct. I think people do conflate gender with genitals. As I always like to say, when a child is born, nobody asks them what their gender is. People just assign it to them. So I think what's striking to me is, yes, for the majority of people that works, meaning that most people can conflate their gender identity with their genitals. But for people who can't or who don't wish to, namely transgender people, in a sense you're stuck with that identity. And it's really difficult to persuade people that your gender identity can be opposite to what your genitals are.

JOE: There also seems to be confusion between sexual orientation issues and gender identity issues.

DR. MASSARELLA: Yes, we tend to not use the term "transsexual" any more because people hear the word and they think of sexual orientation and not gender identity. So I think it is important to make the point that a transgender person can be straight, bi or queer and that their sexual orientation is indeed separate from their identity.

JOE: Exactly, that being transgender does not necessarily presume any particular sexual orientation, but there does seem to be a false association between being transgendered and sexuality, which leads to paranoid fears about transgender women being in men's rooms—in addition, to the fact that the people who claim to be fearful are asserting the ignorant and bigoted view that transgender women are really men.

DR. MASSARELLA: Mm-hmm.

JOE: Of course, there is also the old equation of being gay or transgendered with being more likely to be interested in children sexually, for which there is absolutely no basis in fact.

DR. MASSARELLA: Exactly, and I do make the point that if we were really concerned about safety in bathrooms, why wouldn't we ban priests from bathrooms? Why wouldn't we ban teachers from bathrooms? Because we in fact know that people in these groups have been convicted of assaulting children.

JOE: Yes, and of course you made the point in your TEDx talk on deception that, no, we wouldn't want to do that because we don't want to label people as dangerous because they just happen to be a member of a particular group, but that is exactly what is happening with regard to transgender people. Now there is also a whole socio-economic side to this story as well, which is that although transgender folks tend to be better educated, more of them as a percentage are actually living in poverty, so they also may not be able to afford medical care, or maybe don't have health insurance, at least in the United States.

DR. MASSARELLA: In Canada the issue is usually in seeking treatment because we do have universal health care, so most transgender clients can actually access cross gender hormone therapy, and it doesn't cost them any money other than the cost of drugs. But where we do have that problem is in surgery. In most provinces in Canada transgender surgeries aren't covered. And they're far out of reach of the average trans person.

JOE: Yes, it's astronomically expensive. Another issue, though, is that a lot of trans people who don't want to go to a physician and acknowledge that they're transgender self-medicate. And even though there is accurate information on the web about how to transition and you can order your own tests, that's also extremely expensive as well. So if you did have insurance, maybe it would be paid for, but if you self-medicate, it obviously isn't. So there are really a host of problems. But

I know that you're also optimistic, and you see that we are making progress in a variety of ways. Could you say with reference to your own practice where you see progress?

DR. MASSARELLA: Sure, there are two really striking things. One is that the number of younger people presenting to clinics worldwide has increased dramatically in the last decade, which I think speaks to both a greater awareness of transgender identity and a greater acceptance. Secondly, I've also noticed a very dramatic change over the last few years in the attitude of parents. Four or five years ago parents would come to me and say, "Cure my child," meaning make them not transgendered. Today parents are actually coming to me and saying, "Support my child." That is really just an incredible change in a very short period of time. So what I'm finding is that overall in society, the idea of a transgender identity isn't as unusual as it used to be. I mean, before, there was no transgender middle class. They were either celebrities or sex workers. What we're seeing today is sort of the rise of the transgender middle class. And I think that's a unique phenomenon, and I think it sort of follows the queer community by about ten to twenty years. I think it's really very hopeful.

JOE: That's very important, and I think that there's also more support for families. I had the privilege of speaking last week with Aidan Key as part of The Human Agenda project. He's a transgender man, and he works with transgender children and their families in a program in Seattle called "Gender Diversity," which you may be familiar with.

DR. MASSARELLA: Yes.

JOE: Aidan works with very young children. And it was interesting to talk to him about the whole issue of dysphoria. He told me that there are some very, very young children who, right after they learn to speak, will say, "I'm a girl," even though they were born with a penis. And of course parents are going to think that a child that young is confused.

DR. MASSARELLA: Yes, exactly.

JOE: Aidan also said even if children identify as transgender at a slightly later age, say, five or six when they're going to kindergarten or first grade, that they get no support whatsoever. So you see that the so-called dysphoria or discomfort or feeling bad about one's self is really almost a necessary outcome of their not being supported at such an early age. But now with programs like Aidan's, and with other resources, that could change, and he testifies to the fact that these children thrive once they are supported.

DR. MASSARELLA: Yes, I often talk about the pseudo-psychiatric diagnosis that accompanies the diagnosis of gender dysphoria. You'll see kids who come to you who are diagnosed with anxiety, OCD, personality disorder, ADD, Asperger's. And I think a lot of these diagnoses are just pseudo-psychiatric diagnoses for gender dysphoria, and in fact if we address the heart of the issue, which as you say is really a gender incongruence, then I think a lot of the time we won't see any of these so-called psychiatric diagnoses. Instead we'll see really healthy children who are leading productive and fulfilling lives. I often have clients who see me at quite a young age. And by the time we're finished, they're no longer on an anti-depressant. They're no longer on an anti-psychotic. They're living quite happily. So it strikes me as quite common. In fact, last week I received a referral for a three year old, which I think is really encouraging.

JOE: That is encouraging, and I was encouraged as well by the fact that you work at a Catholic teaching hospital, so we're seeing institutional support, even within the Catholic hospital community, for transgender clients and for physicians who treat them. It is just so important to have all of these changes in place to be able to move forward with transgender rights and to be able to achieve freedom and equality for all transgender people.

DR. MASSARELLA: I couldn't agree with you more. Which is why it's important to be out. We've talked for years about why it's important for queer people to be out, even if you can live by stealth. If you come out and aren't afraid and people accept you, then for the next generation of people, you take away the power of people who create fear. It takes courage sometimes to be out, but at the end of the day it's the right thing to do, so I always applaud trans people who are willing to speak up. It takes a lot of bravery. I am a very privileged transperson. I didn't lose my life. I didn't lose my job. I didn't lose my family. But that being said, I still have an obligation, I think, to speak up and to make things better.

JOE: Of course, the more people who come out, the more support there is for everybody else to come out. Do you have any new projects or new initiatives that you are planning that you would like to share?

DR. MASSARELLA: Yes. One is that our national broadcaster in Canada, the CBC, is doing a documentary about trans people, which I will likely participate in. Also, we're looking at doing a trial at all the major sites in Canada where we treat transgender children to look at outcomes. We're looking forward to that.

JOE: Those are really exciting projects. You are doing tremendous work. As I said at the outset, it's an honor to speak with you. And I thank you for giving me a few minutes today.

DR. MASSARELLA: Well, thank you, Joe, very much.

Y-LOVE (YITZ JORDAN)

"You can only have unity through diversity. Otherwise, it's just homogeneity. When two disparate things come together, that's when we have unity."

Y-Love (aka Yitz Jordan) is a hip hop artist. He's also an Orthodox Jew and is known as the first African American Orthodox Jewish MC. Y-Love grew up in a Christian household but was attracted to Judaism at an early age. He became a Hasidic Jew in the year 2000 and went on to study at a yeshiva in Jerusalem. In 2001 he began performing hip hop at open mikes in New York City, displaying a unique, multi-lingual style that incorporates English, Hebrew, Yiddish, Arabic and Aramaic. In 2005, he released *DJ Handler Presents Y-Love: The Mixtape*. In 2008, released his first full-length album, *This is Babylon*. He has said that his music embodies Jewish values and appeals to an audience of conservative-minded hip hop fans. In 2012 he came out as gay. In addition to being a hip hop artist, Y-Love is also an LGBTQ activist and a writer. His writing has appeared in the *Huffington Post, Quartz,* the *Advocate* and the *Jewish Post*.

JOE: Welcome! It's really a pleasure to have a chance to chat with you, Y-Love.

Y-LOVE: Good to talk to you.

JOE: Before we get into exploring your very interesting and unique journey through music and religious belief, I was wondering if you could talk a little bit about something that I think is very important. It's really the central message, as I understand it, of your music, which to me is summed up in your song and your video called "This is Unity."

Y-LOVE: Exactly.

JOE: You're really about celebrating unity while at the same time embracing difference and diversity. So could you just talk a little bit about that?

Y-LOVE: Exactly. At its core my music is hip hop that's about making the world a better place. I tell people at all of my shows, why is the question. Love is the answer—that all of our actions should be motivated by a sense of love, a sense of a common, shared agenda, a sense of unity. You can only have unity through diversity. Otherwise, it's just homogeneity. When two disparate things come together, that's when we have unity. So by celebrating unity, you're ultimately celebrating diversity at the same time. I use hip hop as a way to build bridges between people. I say that all bridges help to build the world, and all walls put up between people help to destroy the world. It's just that simple. If we want to have cohesive communities, if we want to have a positive future, if we want to see humanity prosper, we're going to have to put aside as many conflicts as possible.

JOE: You've really been about diversity from the beginning. When you were very young, you were attracted to Judaism, which is a different set of values and a different culture from what one might encounter in a Christian household in America. I'm just wondering, what attracted you to the beliefs and to the values of Judaism.

Y-LOVE: My very first exposure to anything Jewish was when I was seven years old and I saw a commercial on TV that said "Happy Passover from your friends at Channel 2." *I started* drawing the six-pointed star that I saw on the commercial on everything in my mother's house. I didn't know anything about Judaism at the time. It was kind of an instinctive attraction. I understood that there was a group of people called Jews and I had to become one of them, whatever that meant. My grandmother actually wanted to be Jewish her entire life. During the times of segregation, the colored community and the Jewish community in Baltimore had one thing in common. The same people who didn't like colored people also didn't like Jews. So the colored community and the Jewish community had a symbiotic relationship for a long time. When I first decided that I had an interest in Judaism as a small child, my grandmother brought me my first yarmulke. When I was about nine and I said I didn't want to celebrate Christmas anymore, she brought me my first menorah. When I was about fourteen, I started going to services at Johns Hopkins University's Jewish Student Center and taught myself how to read Hebrew, literally got a learn to read Hebrew children's book from the library and began sounding out the alphabet. It was a self-propelled discovery process. It's not that I knew about the beliefs of Judaism and then thought, wow, this resonates with me. It was more like, I know that I want to be Jewish, so let me find out what I believe.

JOE: So there was kind of an instinctive attraction, and you felt a sense of solidarity early on, and you had some support from your family, and then you began studying and exploring as a young boy.

Y-LOVE: Right.

JOE: When did you first become aware of your sexual orientation? And at that point, did you see any potential conflicts between your attraction to Judaism and being gay?

Y-LOVE: For every chronological point in my Jewish journey, there's a similar chronological point in realizing my sexual orientation. My first time having a crush on a boy would be around second grade, just about the same time that I realized that I was interested in Judaism. I felt instinctively that I was in the closet from then—from the time that I realized that I liked boys and not girls. I realized that was something I had to keep quiet. I came out to my mother at thirteen. And she was not supportive at all, very verbally abusive. We would have fights for hours. And so that would be kind of the baggage that I would take to learning about Judaism. But I didn't really see too much of a conflict at the time, especially because there are 613 commandments in the Torah and if you tell me that I'm only keeping 612, well no one is perfect. So if you're gay and you're not keeping that commandment, well fine, just keep the Sabbath a little bit more scrupulously or make sure that your kosher observance is high or things like that. Over time, I realized the severity of the infraction, the transgression, and by the time I was 21 and was in the process of converting, I kind of had to put my gay side behind me, so to speak. I tried to just sublimate all the feelings that I had towards other guys. I would just put that into Torah learning. I would just channel all of that into Jewish observance and try to pray the gay away, for lack of a better term.

JOE: So like many LGBTQ people, you felt pressured to stay in the closet for many reasons. It wasn't just Judaism but your mother's response or perhaps your family's response or perhaps a friend's. I'm wondering, in that context, what about hip hop and the hip hop community, which is also not necessarily known for embracing the LGBTQ community. How did you feel about your interest in hip hop in relation to your identity as a gay guy?

Y-LOVE: I'll preface this by saying that growing up, I wasn't really into hip hop as a style of music. I grew up listening to punk rock and heavy metal and hard rock. So I was fortunate to have a really supportive group of progressive friends who were always around me in school and always around me at concerts. Also, I went to a magnet school and was saved from a lot of the anti-gay bullying that I would have been exposed to if I had gone to my neighborhood school. That being said, hip hop for me at that age was just something that I would do as a hobby. When my friends and I would get together, maybe we would come up with a few rhymes. Everyone knew that if you were gay, you were persona non grata in the hip hop scene. Going to the hip hop shows, being part of the hip hop community and the hip hop culture wasn't really an option. I didn't really pursue hip hop as an art form until I studied at a yeshiva in Israel. That's when I started listening to underground hip hop and started actually honing my rhyming skills and going to hip hop shows. Actually I didn't go to hip hop shows until I was Orthodox. Just because if I had that gay identity, I didn't belong there, so it was only a place for me to be in the closet.

JOE: And that's where you developed your multilingual lyrical style, using it as a kind of mnemonic device to help you remember what you were studying in yeshiva, correct?

Y-LOVE: Exactly. The first person I learned Talmud with was an MC from Long Island, and like you said, as a mnemonic device we would use hip hop. The Talmud is written in Aramaic, so that's where my Aramaic skills came from—just from those days of learning Talmud back and forth freestyle. And because we were learning in Israel, that's where the Hebrew came in. And because I was Hasidic at the time, of course, I had to learn Yiddish as a part of the conversion process. So Yiddish would work its way into the flow as well. In my lyrics, I didn't feel like I could express everything that I wanted to say in English. So I began using as many languages as I could.

JOE: So those studies liberated you as a writer and really influenced your style as a hip hop artist?

Y-LOVE: Definitely. If it had not been for those days in *yeshiva,* none of this would be happening. Yeshiva and the whole Jewish learning process is what made me a hip hop artist.

JOE: You were Hasidic, and now you're Orthodox, what prompted that change?

Y-LOVE: Well, I guess I consider myself now to be more ex-Orthodox than Orthodox. You know, still observant to some degree but not nearly as much as I was before. As to the reason I left the Hasidic world—well, I had an arranged marriage in 2003 to a Hasidic woman, which only lasted about four months. After that, matchmakers started going around seeing if they could find a match for Yitz, because it seemed that everyone had a black friend. In 2005, someone tried to set me up with the cousin of one of the members of my sect, and he had apparently heard rumors that I was gay. So he went to Gay Pride armed with his digital camera to take pictures and get proof that I was gay. That would be the year that I would actually go to Gay Pride, having been talked into it by one of my friends and the guy who I was dating at the time. So I decided to go with much trepidation to the parade. And there was the guy from my sect, taking pictures of me. He took a few hundred pictures of me down to my rabbi in Brooklyn in an effort to get my conversion invalidated. I didn't get excommunicated, nor was my conversion invalidated, but at that point I already was alienated from the community because I didn't know who had seen the pictures or who knew what. I basically was a recluse for a few years after that. For me, the Hasidic community went from being this warm, open place where there was much less racism and much more acceptance of diversity to being a place where I didn't know who was my friend and who wasn't. So in 2009, I felt I had to leave the Hasidic world basically for my own sanity.

JOE: When you decided to come out, you must have felt some trepidation not only with reference to the Hasidic and Orthodox communities but the hip hop community as well.

Y-LOVE: Right. When I left the Hasidic community, I started to come out to my friends in my social circle, 75% of whom probably already knew at the time. But that started this dichotomy where Yitz Jordan was gay, but Y-Love wasn't. So whereas most rappers, if they're on tour, go out to the club or have fun with their friends, I would go back from the club to the hotel room and see if I could find somebody gay to talk to online. It created this sense that I was alienating myself from myself. I couldn't be myself anywhere. I couldn't let anyone know that I was Y-Love. Once actually when I was on tour in Israel, someone saw me in a gay bar in Tel Aviv, and he said, "Aren't you Y-Love?" And I ran into the bathroom. I had to keep those worlds separate. That's not productive, and that really started to take away from the art, started to take away from the creativity, just the stress of having to maintain a closeted public identity at the same time as an out private one. I couldn't deal with that, living in two worlds, so by 2012, for my own sanity I had to come out. I wrote a tear-filled coming out article, which would eventually get excerpted on Out.com and in the *Advocate*. In the article I said I wanted to eventually get married and have a family and that could only be possible with a man. I said I had to be myself.

I was expecting an extreme homophobic backlash. That's why I moved to California. I was terrified. I figured that there was going to be angry Hasidic people with pitchforks at my door.

JOE: You feared the backlash.

Y-LOVE: Yeah. Of course, that's not what happened.

JOE: Yes, you've gotten tremendous support, and it's opened up all sorts of new avenues for you and, as you know, positioned you now as an LBGTQ activist.

Y-LOVE: Yeah. I came out professionally through a video called "Focus on the Flair," where it's not only me appearing with a Hasidic actor but also me in drag, just my way of visually coming out to all my fans. When the article and my video appeared on Out.com, it got about 10,000 shares on Facebook. There were comments from yeshiva kids who were living in Israel at the time, and the gist was: I don't understand what he just did, but I got to respect him. I don't understand what this video is, but I respect Y-Love. And I started to get messages from kids in communities like Crown Heights, Williamsburg, very traditional Hasidic communities, who said that I gave them the courage to come out to their mom, come out to their sister, come out to their brother, things like that. After that I performed at Pride 2012, and one of my friends from yeshiva said that he not only wanted to march with me, he wanted to go onto the float with me. The gay and lesbian yeshiva day school alumni put a little "Frequently Asked Questions" thing online, telling ultra-Orthodox people where it would be family friendly for them to stand, and you had Hasidic women marching behind the float. I had never imagined that would be the reaction of the ultra-Orthodox community. Now granted, there are still a lot of negative

reactions out there, and I'm definitely not welcomed everywhere. But the fact that there was such an outpouring of support just blew my mind.

JOE: That's really great. It seemed to me too, that in "Focus on
the Flair," you were expressing an identification with the ballroom scene.

Y-LOVE: Oh, yes. When I was about 15, I started voguing, and I was
introduced to the ballroom scene. I would try my hand at
walking femme queen and banji girl and the various drag cat-
egories. But again, that was something that I realized I had to
be in the closet about. But I always liked the style of music,
and I always loved the style of dance. And I expressed that in
"Focus on the Flair."

JOE: So now that you've really come out and expressed who you
are, there must be a whole new set of possibilities for you as
a musician, as a writer, as an activist. What are some of the
upcoming projects that you're working on and we'll all know
about soon?

Y-LOVE: Well, my next album coming out is called "Evolve."
I started writing this album at the end of my living in the
Hasidic world. So it's really the story of my journey. Also,
my coming out process is the subject of a documentary film
called "Y-Love," scheduled to be released soon. And, as a result of being out, I became the spokesperson for Keshet, the
grassroots organization. I speak at events for them. Before
I came out, my speeches revolved around my Jewish journey. Now my speeches are more about coming to terms with
being gay in the Jewish world, coming out and the reaction
after that. Also, a lot of the material that I write for *Quartz*
focuses on gay issues in business and marketing, including
homophobia.

JOE: What about live performances?

Y-LOVE: Since coming out, I've started to see gay MCs at my shows. I'm also noticing kids with yarmulkes on in the audience nodding their heads to gay-themed lyrics, which is something that I just would not have expected.

JOE: Well that's really revolutionary. You are reaching and influencing young people who are attracted to hip hop and who are Jewish, and I think it's all because of your embrace of unity and diversity, which was really the first thing that we talked about and maybe is an explanation for your attraction to Judaism to begin with. You really have an amazing story. It's an evolving story, and I thank you for spending a few minutes with me. I wish you the best of luck.

Y-LOVE: I wish you all the best and let me finish by saying to everybody out there, it does not just get better. It gets awesome.

DR. MARK MAXWELL AND TIMOTHY YOUNG

"The attitudes about families are shifting. Our neighbors think of us as a family. Our neighbors trust their children to be in our home as we trust our children to be in their home. We're just two guys who are working and trying to protect our family."

Dr. Mark Maxwell and Timothy Young are true advocates for equality. They stand up for themselves and for their children every single day and by virtue of that they are standing up for everyone in the LGBTQ community as well. Mark and Tim have been together for more than two decades. In 2013 they were married in Washington, DC. However, their marriage was not legally recognized in the state of North Carolina where they live. They are also the parents of four beautiful boys. But again, because of the laws of North Carolina, they were not both allowed to be the parents of their boys. North Carolina does not allow second-parent adoption for same sex couples. Mark and Tim have communicated the story of their parenting and their relationship in a video that is sponsored by Freedom To Marry and is called "A Tale of Two Dads."

AUTHOR'S NOTE: My conversation with Mark and Tim took place on March 11, 2014. At that time the state of North Carolina banned same-sex marriage and also prohibited gay couples from securing second-parent adoption rights. Happily, on

October 10, 2014, the US District Court ruled that the state of North Carolina's ban on same-sex marriage is unconstitutional, thus making marriage equality a reality in North Carolina. Nevertheless, North Carolina continues to deny second-parent adoption rights to same sex-couples. I have included our original conversation in The Human Agenda because it eloquently expresses the injustice of same-sex couples being denied the right to marry. It also communicates the fears and the heartbreak that same-sex couples experience in being denied second-parent adoption rights. I have included a later conversation with Mark and Tim after the same-sex ban in North Carolina was declared unconstitutional to get their reaction to the ruling along with an update on their marital and parental status.

JOE: Mark and Tim, great to talk to you today. Mark, congratulations on receiving your Ph.D. in Public Policy and Administration from Walden University.

MARK/TIM: Thank you, Joe.

JOE: My understanding is that it is possible as a single parent to adopt in North Carolina and that three of your boys were adopted in North Carolina, so in that case sexual orientation was not an issue, but crazily, you cannot adopt as a couple. One partner cannot adopt the children of the other partner. Do I have that right? It just seems insane.

MARK: Yes, you are correct. Tim and I intentionally disclose ourselves as illegal parents of our four boys. We simply say we are parents. We both love our kids, and we are battling them on the same issues that any other parent is battling. We're going through the process of skinny jeans, and you're not going out past a certain time at night—all those things that any other couple deals with. Our reality is like any other family out there, and we want to make sure that our children are protected from anything that could possibly face them--our deaths, perhaps, or God forbid if we split. Half of all marriages end in divorce. That's not something that we see for ourselves, but there is a reality that couples face.

JOE: Well, it's terrible that the fact of your parenthood isn't recognized, and as you were just suggesting, there are some real repercussions in terms of your children being protected as a result of the fact that both of you are not recognized as parents. To put it simply, the partner who is not legally recognized as a parent has no rights or obligations to the children

MARK: Exactly. The issue of second-parent adoption presents some very serious questions. What if something happened to me? What's going to happen to my children? What's going to happen to Tim? We started to really do some homework, and I realized that I wasn't the only one who was asking these questions, so when I enrolled as a doctoral student, I decided to do a study that examined some of these questions. I looked at the topic of second-parent adoption in North Carolina, and I asked same-sex couples to describe their experience adopting a child from foster care. There are the legal issues, which you just touched on. The children lose the protection of having two legal parents.

TIM: If the legal parent dies, then the children are legally orphans. That is obviously a terrible outcome for the children, and it is heartbreaking for the surviving partner as well.

MARK: Yes. Also, families do not feel like full citizens of the state. They feel disenfranchised. There is also an issue if a child has special needs. LGBT couples often adopt children with special needs. We are the island of misfit toys. We take those children that others don't want. We protect them. We love them, and we nurture them. The problem is that children with special needs only have access to special services and health care through the legally recognized parent.

JOE: So the problems really are similar to the challenges that you face if you're not legally married, with one partner not even having the right to visit the other partner in a hospital or have any inheritance rights. There are a whole host of issues raised by your not being recognized legally as a parent.

MARK: That is correct. Nevertheless, we are hopeful. We are on a journey in our country. We believe deeply in our Constitution and the values of our country. Prior to June 2013, we had no recognition as a married couple on the federal level. Now the federal government says to us, "You are recognized." This year for the first time we filed a joint tax return. For us, it was less about the economics of it. It was really more symbolic of the fact that we had the right to do that.

TIM: It was amazing when we were actually legally married. I mean we had been together for over two decades, and now we were finally married like everybody else.

MARK: Now the difficult part to deal with is that we are legal strangers to each other in our home state. We own homes together. We have run a business together. We raise children together. But we're considered legal strangers. We spend lots of money to make sure that we protect each other, and that we protect our children. But there's always that little thing in the back of our minds that basically says, "What if?" What if someone decides to challenge this will or challenge the power of attorney?

JOE: It's just so offensive that people deny facts that are staring them in the face: that you are a married couple, that you are the parents of your children. And it's even more disturbing when they state platitudes that they think prove their case like, "Children do best with a mother and a father," as if there are no exceptions to that. Obviously there are numerous exceptions with respect to children being raised by a mother and a father. There could be abuse in the family. There could be mental illness issues, substance abuse issues. The incontrovertible truth is not that children do best with a mother and a father but that they do best when they're loved--and they can be loved by two men or two women. We know it's difficult as single parents to raise children, but some children do extremely well with single parents. I'm a single parent myself. And so, I think that we need to get to the point where people just recognize these human facts, and I'm wondering now: Is there progress being made with respect to the adoption laws in North Carolina, and also now that the Defense of Marriage Act has been declared unconstitutional, what about the prospects for your marriage to be recognized in North Carolina?

MARK: Unfortunately, it's a slow process in our home state. But we have some of the most amazing people who live in this state. We are shifting. The attitudes about families are shifting. Our neighbors think of us as a family. Our neighbors trust their children to be in our home as we trust our children to be in their home. We're just two guys who are working and trying to protect our family.

JOE: Absolutely.

MARK: We do have legislators in Raleigh who make conscious decisions to put forth bills and to push through laws—

TIM: Policies—

MARK: Policies that are basically discriminatory. They are not only discriminatory toward the LGBTQ community but toward women and minorities as well.

TIM: I think ultimately it'll take change on the federal level before the laws in North Carolina really change.

JOE: The interesting thing to me, though, is that after the DOMA ruling, Antonin Scalia of all people said that because of the breadth of the decision, he felt that if couples who are married in one state moved to a state that denied the right of same-sex marriage and they took that case to court that they would in fact win. Are you aware of any people in the state of North Carolina who are taking legal action to overturn the state law prohibiting same-sex marriage?

MARK: The ACLU has filed a lawsuit against the state of North Carolina on behalf of six couples and their children for second-parent adoption. Once the 2013 decision was made in the Windsor case, that lawsuit was amended to include marriage equality.

JOE: Could you talk a little bit about your concept of family? You are such loving and proud parents. Your children are beautiful, and yet there are people who continue to denigrate the idea of two men or two women raising families. In fact, I wrote a piece for the *Huffington Post* about how there are so many organizations who use the word "family" in their name who are actually anti-gay hate groups. When they use the word "family," these groups are actually trying to co-opt the word and redefine "family" as an exclusively heterosexual unit, in fact to assert that gay, lesbian and transgender people don't even have the right to form families, don't have the right to adopt children, to be parents, and to lead children in the community. You are proof that that is false. You're human beings who love your children, and you're the same as anyone else raising a family. What is the meaning of "family" to you?

TIM: We came together initially and built a great foundation, and then we wanted to expand what our family looked like. I can definitely say we are not perfect people.

JOE: Who is? Nobody's perfect.

TIM: Right. We're like everybody else, and our kids are just like other kids. They really just want to be safe and be well taken care of. To answer your question, I would say that we are people who came together under one roof for a common purpose, and that is to grow and evolve and to love each other unconditionally.

MARK: For us, the meaning of family has evolved so much.

TIM: We have friends that are really close to us that we definitely consider to be family. They have bonded with us, and we trust them implicitly.

MARK: Right. We had a situation recently where power was out for several days in our home and in our community. And there was never a question. There were people who said, "You're staying with us. This is how this is going to go." So that's family to us.

JOE: What about support within your families growing up and when you first came together? In addition to being a gay couple, you are also an interracial couple. Did you have support from your families for your relationship?

MARK: In those days, people were just becoming aware of HIV/ AIDS, and they linked that to gay men, and they said "OK, if you're gay, you're going to die." So unfortunately for a number of years, we had to walk through this kind of cloud in terms of educating our families that it was possible for two men to be in a relationship, to care for each other and to live a healthy life together.

TIM: I can honestly say, as a white person, being with Mark has evolved my soul and my life experience so much. It's one of the greatest gifts of my life. Talking about our families and when we first started out, it's been a process. Like everybody else, we have things that we're working through. We have amazing blessings in our lives, and then we have challenges in our lives. My parents loved Mark. At the same time, we have family members on both sides of the challenge. We still have those conversations, and they are part of an ever-evolving thing.

MARK: When we planned our wedding in the District of Columbia, we sent invitations to our family and friends. And many of them were there to support us. But I had a white family member who chose not to attend. What was communicated to me directly was, "We don't believe in same-sex marriage." So it's pretty rude, pretty direct, and sometimes that's hurtful to Tim. With respect to those who choose not to support us as a couple, as a family, I'm OK with that. We're OK. We focus on nurturing and giving back to our community any way that we can. That's all that we can do.

JOE: It's amazing how positive you remain. It's obvious that it is a struggle. But I think that it's encouraging that peoples' hearts and minds do change. And the support that you do get from your family, though it's not from everyone, and from the neighborhood and the community is a testimony to that. It shows that people are ahead of the law, and we see that everywhere these days, and so that is something to really be optimistic about.

MARK: I feel that we are on a positive course nationally, and I want to hold out hope that our legislators will do the right thing on behalf of all LGBTQ couples in this country.

TIM: We want to spread equality around rural America. We feel like we have a responsibility--that we are now legally married, and we want to help others have that.

MARK: It breaks our hearts, as a couple, to hear what is happening, for example, in Uganda, where couples are being paraded down the streets and being attacked and killed. We feel that we need to bring that situation into the light.

JOE: When you bring up Uganda, I think that makes the point that with progress there's always a backlash. It's disturbing that there are people on the Religious Right from this country who actually went to Uganda and were advocating for those laws that are so inhumane and that violate basic human rights. That's why it is so important for all of us to stand up in our own lives every single day and just be who we are. That to me is true activism—when you are representing what freedom and equality mean in your own lives.

MARK: Tim and I have very open discussions about pretty much everything. And race is one of the things we talk about. Three of our boys are bi-racial, and one is Caucasian. So for us, diversity is a very important issue, and we look for it everywhere—in an advertisement in an LGBTQ publication to anything that's happening within our community. We always ask, OK, where is the diversity? Are we seeing our diverse population? I attended the LGBT in the South Conference recently, in Asheville, North Carolina, and there were approximately 250 people from various areas of the South who were present, and some from other areas of the country. It was a fantastic time. And one of the questions posed was "Where are the African Americans in this struggle?" One of the ladies said, "In the sixties, I marched for civil rights for African Americans, where are they?" And I had to say that this is a journey for many African Americans. You need to first understand the journey that we took through civil rights, and you need to understand that the church within the black community is the foundation for many African Americans. So, when

I walk into a family gathering, I know that there are family members who greet me unconditionally, but I also know that there are family members that in the back of their minds are saying, "Yeah, I love him, but he's going to hell."

JOE: Right. And you shared in one of your interviews that a family member had said, "I love you, but I have a problem with your lifestyle." I think it's interesting that if you're heterosexual that sexual orientation doesn't seem to be part of your lifestyle, right? Your lifestyle is your work and your hobbies and so forth, but if you are gay or lesbian or transgender, suddenly sexual orientation and gender identity are a lifestyle. When people make remarks like that, you need to question what the depth of that love really is.

TIM: Mm-hmm.

MARK: That is true. I look at my siblings and my friends, and I see them as these wonderful beings, and I also see that we all have certain flaws that we struggle with day in and day out, whether we're struggling with a body image or a psychological issue or mental illness, or whatever it is. We're all on this journey working through something, and I think the less we judge whatever it is that we're seeing in another person and the more we try to get additional information on what they're going through, the more we can see them in a new light. For example, our 16 year old is very artistic, very creative.

TIM: Yes, he identifies as gay, and there are some things that kids do today that as gay people we may not have done years ago. For example, if he wants to carry a purse to school or wear a certain type of clothing, we even as gay people have to say, "Wow, OK. I have to process that. Let me understand what's going on in my own head." So we're always evolving.

MARK: We are always evolving, and he in particular is teaching us to understand that he is this unique being. He's a very creative, very free flowing spirit, and each day is a little different. And as a gay teen, at 16 years old, he has this remarkable grasp on what is really happening, and we're very proud of him.

JOE: It's great how we learn from our children, and to your point: if we can just be open minded and learn from one another and stop judging, then I think we can get over some of these conflicts that are dividing us.

MARK: Absolutely.

JOE: Well, I want to thank both of you so much for taking this time to talk with me. Your story's inspiring. I'm a father of three children, and I admire your parenting skills, your pride in your family, and your love for your children. I think that you're both shining examples of what it means to be loving parents and loving spouses, so thank you once again so much for taking this time with me today.

MARK/TIM: Thank you, Joe.

Update from Mark and Tim, January 12, 2015

JOE: Hey, Mark and Tim. I wanted to get back together with both of you to give you the opportunity to share your reactions to the U.S. District Court's ruling that the state of North Carolina's ban on same-sex marriage is unconstitutional, which, of course, made marriage equality a reality in North Carolina. How did that feel?

TIM: It felt amazing. I felt so many emotions inside of myself.

MARK: It was definitely a sense of elation, seeing what happened in Virginia and other states and then getting the news of the U.S. District Court's decision in North Carolina.

JOE: Yes, since the Supreme Court refused on October 6 to review appeals in five states to overturn lower court rulings that legalized same-sex marriage, 17 states have legalized it—most recently Florida—bringing the total to 36 states that have legalized same-sex marriage.

TIM: That's right. And we see the work that our friends at the Campaign for Southern Equality and Freedom to Marry are doing. We know the people who are working so hard there for couples and families in Mississippi and other states, and we're extremely proud of them.

MARK: We actually traveled to Mississippi with the Campaign for Southern Equality and did an event there with them. It was amazing. Each place that you go, everyone's focused on the same goal, and you get to meet people, and you listen to their real life stories.

JOE: It's wonderful to share in all of that. I was wondering, too. What is your marital status in the state of North Carolina now that marriage equality is a reality there?

TIM: We are now legal. We actually recorded our marriage license in October 2014.

JOE: Congratulations, that's really exciting. I also wanted to ask you about the other major issue that we discussed in our original conversation. It was the fact that North Carolina also prohibited same-sex couples from second-parent adoption so that only the biological or adoptive parent has legal status. That meant in your case that Mark was recognized as the father of your boys, but you, Tim, didn't have the legal status of being the second parent. What is the current status of your joint parental rights in North Carolina?

MARK: Second-parent adoption has not been resolved at this point. North Carolina still prohibits second-parent adoption for same-sex couples even though we are now legally married in the state. The case is pending. And it is really critical from the perspective of the children who are dangling there in limbo. Second-parent adoption allows the non-biological parent to adopt their partner's children whether or not their marriage is recognized in the state in which they reside and without terminating the parental rights of the other biological parent. Since we are legally married, what we do have is the right to stepparent adoption for the children, which typically requires the consent of the other biological parent unless a court terminates those rights. In dealing with this situation, Tim and I chose early on to do a joint custody agreement. We're looking at this issue from the standpoint of what is the best and most economical option for our family, because there is the issue of cost. A second-parent adoption can cost upwards of $5,000 to complete. When we go into any legal situation with our children, we have our joint custody agreement with us. The joint custody agreement allows Tim to make decisions on behalf of the children, which is important, especially in a situation requiring emergency care.

JOE: So North Carolina is still discriminating against you because you are a same-sex couple by prohibiting Tim from having second-parent adoption status, even though you're married, which seems absurd.

TIM: Absolutely. It's not only discriminating against us. It's definitely discriminating against our children, because the ultimate goal is for them to feel that whatever happens, we're both going to be there for them. It's really important for them to feel safe. They've already had a lot of really crazy stuff happen in their lives.

JOE: What is the prospect for second-parent adoption in North Carolina?

MARK: I think we will have second-parent adoption. It's a matter of walking the course just as we did with the issue of marriage equality and recognizing the rights of same-sex couples. Of course, the issue of same-sex couples having parental rights goes beyond the legal piece of it. At the heart of this is the fact that we're under a microscope day in and day out as gay and lesbian individuals and parents. Anything that happens from the standpoint of our children, whether they're acting out or anything of that nature, how we handle it as parents is looked at in a different way. We certainly feel those challenges, and we attempt to meet those every day. So we recognize that this issue is bigger than the adults involved. This is really a matter of protecting the interests of our kids. And that's worth fighting for.

JOE: Of course, there is nothing more important than that. Let me congratulate you both once again, because it is a joy to know that your marriage is now recognized in North Carolina. And we have reason to believe that second-parent adoption will become a reality as well. We are certainly making progress. I can see a time—perhaps you guys can too--when marriage equality will be a reality in all 50 states. I'm also hoping that we'll soon see the day when there's no question about parental rights or the right to lead children in the community with respect to people who are gay or lesbian or queer or transgender.

TIM: Absolutely. We will prevail. I really believe this. It's exciting to see what's happening. I love to see that same-sex couples, especially young couples, are getting married, and they're starting their families and to see the diversity that is reflected within our community and our families.

MARK: In March of 2014, a national poll showed 59% support for the freedom to marry, a record high. The poll also showed support at 50% or higher in every region of the country. Hopefully this year has made a difference, and support has inched up even more.

JOE: It is very encouraging. Thank you so much for spending this additional time with me so that we can give everybody an update on the happy progress that we are making.

TIM/MARK: Thank you, Joe.

DR. JONIPHER KUPONO **KWONG**

> "I think there's just a greater synergy these days, realizing that we're all human and that love is love and it doesn't matter what gender we happen to fall in love with. What does matter is the quality of the love that we share with each other."

Doctor Jonipher Kupono Kwong is an ordained minister with the Unitarian Universalist Association, and since 2011 he's been the Settled Minister of the First Unitarian Church of Honolulu. Dr. Kwong has a rather ecumenical religious background. He was baptized as a Chinese Mennonite; he's been a member of Evangelical, United Methodist and Episcopalian denominations as well as a member of Calvary Chapel and the Honolulu Mindfulness Community, which is a Zen Buddhist community. He's been extremely active in the marriage equality movement, in California and Hawaii, and very happily, he and Chris Nelson, his partner of 15 years, in December 2013 became the first same-sex couple married in Hawaii.

———————

JOE: I'm delighted to have the chance to speak with you today, Dr. Kwong.

DR. KWONG: Thank you. Likewise.

JOE: I wanted to get started by asking you how you became personally involved in the marriage equality movement. We all have issues that are meaningful to us personally. But it's a big step to become a public activist or to make an issue a focal point of your life. You did that when you were in California and have been doing it in Hawaii as well. What was the motivation and inspiration for that?

DR. KWONG: Well, as an ordained minister, I've always been curious as to how we can live out our fate and how we can walk the walk and not just talk the talk. And so for me looking around and seeing what issue is near and dear to the hearts of members of my congregation, I soon realized that having a sense of equal dignity and inherent worth and respect of every individual is indeed at the core of Unitarian Universalist teachings. So I wanted to explore what that meant further, and naturally it led me to marriage equality since that was what we were voting on in California at the time. And so I quickly became involved in an organization called California Faith for Equality. It was such a delight to work across religious boundaries and work with the Jewish community, the Buddhist community. As you know, I do have quite an ecumenical and interfaith background. So for me it was that intersection between LGBT justice and racial justice and also religious justice and just plain old human rights.

JOE: To me that's really the essence of the struggle. It's about justice and equality. Marriage equality has certainly gained a lot of support in recent years. I'm wondering if you could contrast what you sensed in the earlier days, when you first became involved in California against how you view the situation now. Do you see us moving from mere tolerance or even acceptance to the recognition that everybody deserves full equality with respect to having the right to marry the person they love?

DR. KWONG: Absolutely. It really warms my heart—the rate of progress that we've made in the LGBT community. I wasn't here about two decades ago when this conversation began in Hawaii. I was just finishing off high school. But from what I understand, back then there was so much resistance, especially from certain members of the religious community, and they were bussing people in to go testify and to hold up signs. Not that they've stopped doing that in my view, but I think there's just a greater synergy these days, realizing that we're all human and that love is love and it doesn't matter what gender we happen to fall in love with. What does matter is the quality of the love that we share with each other. I had done a lot of organizing work in Orange County, California, which is not necessarily known as a bastion of liberalism, but even there, there were certainly people who were very committed to phone banking and to talking to their friends and neighbors about just incredible stories of gay people. If you have a grandchild who's gay or a mother who's lesbian or somebody in your family who is a member of the LGBT community, then your thoughts begin to change about it. Ultimately, it starts with the heart and the connection that we have as human beings to one another on that deep and intimate level. That's when people's minds change. That was one of the greatest lessons I learned, the importance of having the courage and the conviction to just tell our stories. After all, as Harvey Milk said, if everyone who is gay or lesbian came out, there wouldn't be homophobia in our society. Of course, it didn't hurt that we had these great public figures like Ellen DeGeneres or great TV shows like "Will and Grace" to help put a face to it in such a public way. But I think humor is very important as well. I think this shows through with your work as well and with other people who are trying to not take it too seriously but at the same time point out that when we share laughter together, we help boost the dignity of each other. When we do that, we learn just to not take life too seriously and perhaps look at certain issues that we're uncomfortable with in a different light.

JOE: Well, you're certainly right that when issues become personal, feelings and emotions change about them. If you have a son or a daughter or a brother or a sister who comes out as gay or lesbian or transgender, you're going to have a better understanding of the issues. That's why it's so important for people to come out, although that puts the burden on the LGBT people. But I've experienced in my own family and a lot of people have too that even when people are close, that religion can get in the way of understanding. So I'm really interested in hearing what you have to say about people who base their condemnation of gay people or lesbians or transgender people on their religious beliefs. How do you interact with those people and try to enlighten them?

DR. KWONG: Well, first of all I also want to say that it's not just the LGBT people themselves who have to come out. It's also the family members. I think of my own mother, for example, who has had to struggle with it over the past 15 years since she's known about my relationship with my now husband and partner. At the same time that she knows that she loves him, she still has to struggle with who she tells about this, and even hanging the family picture on top of the fireplace mantel is a struggle, right? Or saying, "Well, do we really admit who is part of our family? Or do we hide it in the closet?" So I think to that extent even close family members can be quote unquote queer in that they are perceived differently by society when they support LGBT family members. They still have to go through that coming out process. My family being as religious as they are—and as you mentioned, I was raised in an evangelical, fundamentalist Protestant environment—my family certainly hold very strong beliefs about what they believe the Bible teaches or traditionally what the church has espoused. And it's not up to me to change their interpretation of the Bible or whatnot. But for me it has to go to the core of every religious tradition, which in my opinion is about loving one another. It's about showing compassion toward each other, and it's about the Golden Rule—that we treat others as we ourselves would like to be treated. And so what better basis than to say that we're opening our houses of worship and we're celebrating LGBT couples and the commitment that they make to each other because of our religious convictions, because our greatest teacher Jesus taught us to love one another? He never mentioned a peep about LGBT issues. He taught that we should treat all people the same and show compassion for everyone. So if the founder of Christianity has that perspective on what it means to be kind and compassionate to each other, then why can't the followers have a similar perspective? And so that's always been the biggest question in my mind—how to major in the major issues and not the minor ones. And how to not let these minor disagreements get in the way of the bigger picture, which again is at the core of every religion.

JOE: Yes. But there does seem to be deep-seated resistance to what I think you've touched on as the ultimate goal and what is my ultimate goal, which is equality, right? For people to say if you're homosexual, that is as authentic as being heterosexual. If you're transgender, that is as authentic as being cisgender. There's real resistance to that. Some people seem to be able to tolerate or even say I accept you even though I don't approve. But to get to the ultimate goal of embracing equality is still quite a big challenge.

DR. KWONG: It is, and I think it stems from the fact that we're separated from each other and also from the idea that somehow difference equals bad. Certainly the civil rights movement pointed this out—when Dr. King said that we should be judged not by the color of our skin but the content of our character. It highlights the fact that we are all born into this world as human beings and what we do with our lives is what matters. Again it comes down to how we treat each other. That's how we're going to be judged. Are we exhibiting loving acts, or are we hurting one another or being violent towards each other or exhibiting qualities of prejudice and bigotry towards each other? So I think ultimately we need to get rid of that separation and of that negative view of difference—how your color is different from my color and how you grew up in a different family than I grew up in and on the wrong side of the tracks or whatnot. As long as we harbor those kinds of feelings towards each other, we're going to continue to live in a divided world and in a place where we exhibit violence towards each other. But for me, healing relationships is about getting beyond that and looking into how we can work towards the common good—that the good of the community is really going to be our ultimate epic. And the good of the community can only be achieved when we do have justice and equality for all people. That for me again is the moral foundation of my faith.

JOE: It's really about focusing on our common humanity, right? A lot of people just let differences get in the way. In fact, often it seems to be an objection to differences that actually prompts people to be bigoted or to be prejudiced. And so I'm wondering too, how do you deal with the very definition of marriage? Speaking about finding common ground, if we could maybe arrive at a definition of marriage that everybody embraces, that might help tremendously. It seems to me that most people simply want society and the culture that they live in to recognize their committed relationship. Really, it's as simple as that. But people still impose on marriage other requirements, like, well it's got to be a man and a woman raising a family when lots of men and women get together and don't have children, which is quite obvious. Sometimes the facts are obvious, but we still don't really see them. And to your point, if we can simply all find common ground with one another, maybe we can agree to get along and move to a different space. But you seem to be very optimistic that we are indeed moving in that direction.

DR. KWONG: I do. And I do believe that marriage, as an institution, has obviously evolved over the years. It used to be much more patriarchal than it is now, for example, and the man got to have as many wives and mistresses as he wanted. And this wasn't even that long ago. I'm catching up on the show "The Tudors" right now, and I'm looking into the life of Henry VIII and all the drama and intrigue around him. In those days most marriages were not necessarily for romantic reasons. Often they were formed out of convenience or for political alliances or to get a bigger dowry for the family and improve their standard of living. It wasn't until very recently within the past century or so that we began to have these ideas that love enters into the picture of marriage and that romance plays a central role. It's even more recent that we figured out that marriage equality is about equality in marriage, regardless of the genders. You can have an opposite gender relationship that has marriage equality in it in the sense that both people do work at the partnership level, figuring things out together, like how are we going to make ends meet and who's going to take care of the kids. So all of the key issues are in constant negotiation, and there's compromise and communication between the parties. So I believe that these days that's how we view a marriage partnership. It's not just about the rights that you have, but it is about truly respecting each other and the contributions that each person makes to the relationship, to make it thrive and flourish and to make it a safe environment to raise a family in if the couple does decide to raise a family. As you mentioned before, with respect to procreation, I know of an eighty-plus year old couple who recently got married, so they certainly didn't get married because they wanted kids. Marriage is not necessarily about procreation. It's about co-creation of a loving relationship. That's the bottom line of what marriage is about, and so if you look at it that way, then gender does not really matter. Again I think we're staying on a very surface level when we just look at marriage in terms of procreation. I think the other confusion that we have in this society is the difference between a religious marriage and a civil marriage, a marriage the state confers upon its citizens. I tell people that there's a difference between a right, R-I-G-H-T, and a rite, R-I-T-E. A right, R-I-G-H-T is something that the state secures for its citizens. And a rite, R-I-T-E, is something that a religious institution confers upon its congregants. The difference is that one is a blessing, a spiritual blessing and an acknowledgment by the religious community. And the other is simply what we are entitled to as citizens.

JOE: Do you think that across the country more and more people will continue to embrace marriage equality? Do you see a time when the so-called red states will embrace marriage equality, and we have it in all 50 states, or do you think that's still a ways down the road?

DR. KWONG: Well, there are always going to be late bloomers, shall we say, in terms of understanding what marriage equality really means. But I do think that we are moving at a very rapid pace towards acceptance and maybe even acknowledgment and celebration in our communities of LGBT relationships. As with any movement, it does come in waves. With racial equality, for example, we're still dealing with voter's rights issues. And with women's rights, we still have to continually educate people about feminist ideals and what equality means in that setting. So I'm not anticipating that it's just going to be a smooth ride forever and ever, amen. There are going to be bumps along the way, and we're probably going to take one step back somewhere. In the so-called red states, it's going to take a while for them to truly understand what this means. And it may take the Supreme Court finally saying that there's enough momentum and critical mass here that we want to establish marriage equality across the board as the Court did in Loving vs. Virginia in the case of anti-miscegenation laws. Call me an optimist, but I do believe that we have enough momentum in our country to make it legal in all fifty states. And sooner rather than later.

JOE: It's telling that your optimism is tempered by the recognition that when we have progress, there is often a backlash, and that's why we all have to continue to stand up in our own lives in favor of freedom and equality every day. And you certainly do that, Dr. Kwong. So I thank you for your advocacy and activism, and I really appreciate your spending a few minutes to share your thoughts with me today.

DR. KWONG: Thank you Dr. Joe, and thank you for your efforts in making this human rights issue better known. I appreciate what you do as well.

JOE: Well, we all have to do the little bit that we can every day.

DR. KWONG: Absolutely!

JOE: Have a great day and again thanks so much, Dr. Kwong.

DR. KWONG: Thank you. Take care. Aloha.

JOE WENKE is a writer, social critic and LGBTQ rights activist. He is the founder and publisher of Trans Über, a publishing company with a focus on promoting LGBTQ rights, free thought and equality for all people. Wenke received a B.A. in English from the University of Notre Dame, an M.A. in English from Penn State and a Ph.D. in English from the University of Connecticut.

Photo by Gisele Alicea (aka Gisele Xtravaganza)

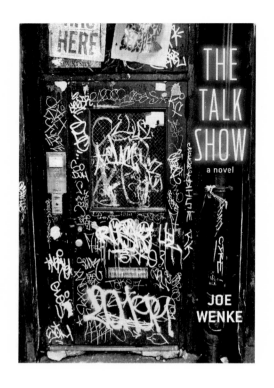

JOE WENKE'S THE TALK SHOW, A NOVEL

Someone is following Jack Winthrop—most likely the gunman who tried to kill America's most controversial talk show host, Abraham Lincoln Jones. Ever since that fateful night when Jones called Winthrop with his audacious proposal, life has never been the same. Winthrop, an award-winning New York Times reporter who calls the Tit for Tat strip club his second home, agreed to collaborate on Jones' national "Emancipation Tour." The plan is to bring Jones' passion for radical change to the people and transcend television by meeting America face to face. Now Winthrop has to survive long enough to make the tour a reality.

As the reach of his stalker spreads, so does the fear that Winthrop's unconventional family is also in danger—Rita

Harvey, the gentle transgender ex-priest and LGBT activist; Slow Mo, the massive vegetarian bouncer; and Donna, stripper and entrepreneurial prodigy—as well as the woman who is claiming his heart, media expert Danielle Jackson.

Steeped in the seamy underbelly of New York City, THE TALK SHOW is a fast-paced and mordantly funny thriller that examines how the forces of nihilism threaten our yearning for love, family and acceptance.

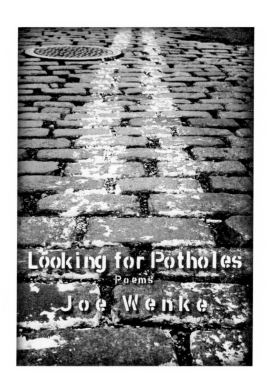

Looking for Potholes

Poems

Joe Wenke

JOE WENKE ON LOOKING FOR POTHOLES
AND FREE AIR

"The poems are very entertaining. Each one is like a little surprise package for the reader to open up. If you enjoy experiencing little epiphanies and revelations about a variety of subjects, including freedom, equality, mortality, troubled relationships, human identity, love and the mysteries of existence, then these poems are for you."

An Ex-Catholic Calls Out the Catholic Church

Papal **BULL**

JOE
WENKE

PRAISE FOR JOE WENKE'S PAPAL BULL

"I may burn in hell for even having read this book."
John C. Wood

"If you enjoyed Wenke's take on the Bible, *You Got to Be Kidding!* read his exegesis of the Catholic Church's past two thousand years. . . . Mordantly funny, scrupulously researched."
E. B. Boatner, Lavender Magazine

"If you wonder why a 'merciful' God created a no-exit-ever hell or if you entertain thoughts of how boring the traditional religious notion of heaven might be, you will meet a savagely witty ally in Wenke's book." *Joe Meyers, CTPost*

"I absolutely LOVED this book. . . . I highly recommend it to any Catholic who is considering recovering from his condition." *Philip G. Harding*

"Joe Wenke is an extraordinary writer. . . . This book is an enlightening journey (for both the author and the reader) that was tenderly written by an exceptional person who is not afraid to let others know about what occurs in so many families, causing a great deal of pain and uncertainty. It is something that should be read by anyone and everyone, regardless of their religion or how they were raised/told by others to believe. There are no words to express the depth of my gratitude to Mr. Wenke and I will be anxiously awaiting any other material that he wishes to write, because I am a lifelong fan." *Jules*

"Ex-Catholics will love this book. It is an amazing satire of the Catholic Church. Every bit as funny as *You Got To Be Kidding!* I highly recommend." *Holly Michele*

"I love this book! It is not only informative but funny as hell." *Rick Martin*

"Funny, clever and spot on." *V. Kennedy*

"Whew! I feel like I've been to confession with the universe, (not God, that's a bad fairytale) and I've been absolved of . . . something. Thank you, Dr. Wenke, for putting into words . . . what I've been thinking about religion, especially Catholicism for a long time. . . . The one thought that kept repeating for me throughout the book, was that I need to buy about 2 dozen copies of this and hand them out to my family members, and at least try to spark a conversation." *Deborah*

"Papal Bull is brilliant and funny, well-researched and informative. . . . [Wenke] writes with humor that is at once scathing, insightful and absurd. His recounting of stories from Catholic grade school made me laugh out loud." *Lori Giampa*

"A cutting, satirical look at Catholic beliefs regarding saints, Mary, birth control, the treatment of women, and of course the huge scandalous cover-up of molestation." *Tiffany A. Harkleroad*

"Impeccably researched and sharply written. . . . [Wenke's] wit and incisive perspective consistently deliver humor and important points to anyone willing to open their minds. . . . A work in which you can think, laugh, and ask the important questions is a must-read." *David Nor*

"For some reason, I kept falling into a George Carlin voice as I read the book." *Joseph Spuckler*

"I love the cover and I love the term 'recovering Catholic' of which I believe I am one. I think any one who went to Catholic School in the fifties and sixties . . . probably had many of the same experiences that the author describes from his school years." *Diane Scholl*

A great and sometimes funny book all 'recovering Catholics' should read. In fact it should be required reading for anybody who considers themselves Holy. Brilliant insight & questions every Catholic should ask themselves." *Robert Kennemer*

"It is necessary to call the church out on their horrendous errors and this book is much needed in society. . . . *Papal Bull* is timely and makes for some very interesting reading. Enjoy!" *Lynda Smock*

"I not only laughed a great deal, but [the book] also gave me a lot to think about." *Michele Barbrow*

"A must read. Excellent!" *Carole*

"This satirical book mocks the church by using actual historical facts. It is a critical and at times humorous analysis of the church's history from a modern perspective." *Katarina Nolte*

"This was a wild ride. I found parts to be rather upsetting but I think the author really did his homework." *Sher Brown*

"An incredibly clever and humorous take on the Catholic Church." *ChristophFischerBooks*

"Wonderfully sacrilegious." *Joe R. Mcauley*

"I absolutely LOVED this book. . . . I highly recommend it to any Catholic who is considering recovering from his condition, and definitely to any atheist, agnostic, or humanist who wants to get the "inside drum" on these religious nutters." *Philip G. Harding*

"A great . . . book all "recovering Catholics" should read. In fact it should be required reading for anybody who considers themselves Holy. Brilliant insight & questions every Catholic should ask themselves." *Robert Kennemer*

"This was a great book. . . . infused with humor and biting wit. It is also a great expose of Catholicism and its many irrationalities and absurdities. As a fellow ex-Catholic who also enjoys calling out the Catholic Church, I can't recommend this book enough." *Alexander*

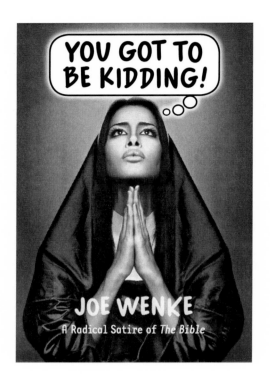

PRAISE FOR JOE WENKE'S
YOU GOT TO BE KIDDING!

"A radically funny book." *Christopher Rudolph, The Advocate*

"Gisele, the notable transgender fashion model, graces the cover. And that image alone challenges the Bible. A transgender woman in a religious pose. . . . Get [*You Got to be Kidding!*] on your Kindle or take it on a trip, the time will fly by—boring this is not!" *Transgenderzone*

"A riotously funny read, I recommend it to anyone who's ever questioned organised religion, especially that of the Bible-bashing, homophobic kind." *Anna, Look!*

"This is hilarious! Joe Wenke gives a nod to Mark Twain as he looks at the Bible with fresh eyes and with the pen of a thinking comic." *Bill Baker*

"This is without a doubt the funniest book I've ever read. I sat with my parents and read aloud some of the passages and we all laughed a lot!" *Emma Charlton, Bookswithemma*

"Very tongue-in-cheek, sarcastic and pointed, dedicated to Christopher Hitchens and Thomas Paine, both of whom would, I believe, really enjoy this book!" *Sarah Hulcey*

"The cover of the book itself is a slap in the face of transphobia. . . . If this book accomplishes one thing, I hope it pushes prejudiced people toward acceptance of LGBT people just as they are." *Isaac James Baker, Reading, Writing & Wine*

"Brave, brilliant and funny. Page after page, biblical chapter after biblical chapter, absurdity after absurdity, this book delivers laugh after laugh. Joe Wenke has crafted the answer to the fundamentalist literal reading of the Bible with the perfect recipe of rationality, candor and humor." *Max Gelt*

"Brilliant . . . for once a funny look at ALL the Bible's insanity." *Jo Bryant*

"Would make a really wicked Christmas present for your Christian friends who have a sense of humor and a sense of the ridiculous." *Ed Buckner, American Atheists*

"Oh my! This is very funny . . . Joe turns everything on its head and makes it a really interesting read." *Stephen Ormsby*

"BEST THING I've READ IN AGES" *Phillip A. Reeves*

"Whether you are an atheist or a Christian who can see the absurdity of some of the anecdotes narrated in Holy Scripture, Joe Wenke's humor won't be wasted on you." *Mina's Bookshelf*

"Great book! Funny and easy to read." *Violets and Tulips*

"Funny and to the point read. Takes a look at the Bible and points out all sorts of inaccuracies, illogical stories and questions. Strongly recommend." *Hertzey*

"Witty and wise. Joe Wenke takes a critical, provocative look at The Bible and he does so with regular hilarity." *Dana Hislop*

"A must-read for anyone who still thinks the Bible is the inviolable word of God—sense of humor mandatory." *K. Sozaeva*

"Such a funny read, my son & I actually read it together! Laughter abounds!" *Rael*

"Deliciously witty!" *Jack Scott*

"Irreverent and hilarious. I am no Bible scholar, but I feel like I have been given the funniest crib notes on this most widely read and probably as widely misunderstood book of all time. I laughed out loud at Wenke's common sense observations and interpretations of this tome." *Lorna Lee*

"Will keep any freethinking reader laughing the whole way through." *George Lichman*

"[*You Got to Be Kidding* is] entertaining and enlightening." *Patti Bray*

"You will be laughing yourself silly while reading this book! In fact, you may find yourself bookmarking a bunch of pages to discuss with your pastor and friends later!" *S. Henke*

"I could not put this book down." *Jackie Hepton*

"This author allows the reader to explore and learn about the Bible with a tongue-in-cheek attitude that keeps you laughing and turning the pages." *Tricia Schneider*

"Some of it made me feel like I might wind up in hell for reading it, but if you keep an open mind and a light heart, you'll have a blast." *Jon Yost*

"Don't read the Bible! Read this!" *Dr. Dan*

"I'm still laughing." *Paul Wilson*

"GREAT. What hogwash we have been fed. Thanks, Joe." *Colin M. Maybury*

"Unforgiving and hilarious." *Phil*

"This book is so funny." *Crystal*

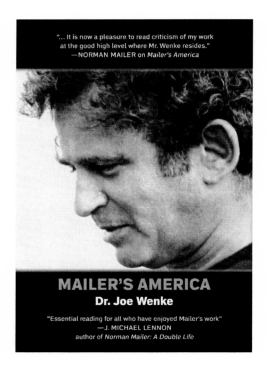

"... It is now a pleasure to read criticism of my work at the good high level where Mr. Wenke resides."
—NORMAN MAILER on *Mailer's America*

MAILER'S AMERICA
Dr. Joe Wenke

"Essential reading for all who have enjoyed Mailer's work"
—J. MICHAEL LENNON
author of *Norman Mailer: A Double Life*

PRAISE FOR JOE WENKE'S MAILER'S AMERICA

The reissue of Joseph Wenke's thoughtful study, *Mailer's America*, provides renewed hope for a deeper understanding of Mailer's work. No other commentator has focused so relentlessly on the deepest purpose of Mailer's hugely varied oeuvre, namely to "clarify a nation's vision of itself." Wenke's examination inhabits, patrols and maps the territory between the millennial promise of America and its often dispiriting actuality. His study contains probing, nuanced and careful examinations of all Mailer's work though the mid-1980s, including one of the first major examinations of Mailer's most demanding novel, *Ancient Evenings*. Wenke's book deserves a wide audience, and is essential reading for all who have enjoyed Mailer's work. —*J. Michael Lennon, author of the authorized biography, Norman Mailer: A Double Life*